I0063252

CREDIT SCORE

Successful Strategies to Build Great Credit and
Increase Your Credit Score

(Your Guide to a Higher Credit Score)

Sidney Gordon

Published by Knowledge Icons

Sidney Gordon

All Rights Reserved

Credit Score: Successful Strategies to Build Great Credit and Increase Your Credit Score (Your Guide to a Higher Credit Score)

ISBN 978-1-990084-77-5

All rights reserved. No part of this guide may be reproduced in any form without permission in writing from the publisher except in the case of brief quotations embodied in critical articles or reviews.

Legal & Disclaimer

The information contained in this book is not designed to replace or take the place of any form of medicine or professional medical advice. The information in this book has been provided for educational and entertainment purposes only.

The information contained in this book has been compiled from sources deemed reliable, and it is accurate to the best of the Author's knowledge; however, the Author cannot guarantee its accuracy and validity and cannot be held liable for any errors or omissions. Changes are periodically made to this book. You must consult your doctor or get professional medical advice before using any of the suggested remedies, techniques, or information in this book.

Upon using the information contained in this book, you agree to hold harmless the Author from and against any damages, costs, and expenses, including any legal fees potentially resulting from the application of any of the information provided by this guide. This disclaimer applies to any damages or injury caused by the use and application, whether directly or indirectly, of any advice or information presented, whether for breach of contract, tort, negligence, personal injury, criminal intent, or under any other cause of action.

You agree to accept all risks of using the information presented inside this book. You need to consult a professional medical practitioner in order to ensure you are both able and healthy enough to participate in this program.

TABLE OF CONTENTS

Introduction

This book contains proven steps and strategies on how to save money and get yourself in better financial shape.

In this book we're going to talk about three different aspects of financial success. We're going to explain how you can and should go about saving more money and what you need to do in order to make sure that you eliminate debt.

Getting yourself in the best possible financial shape is important to your overall success in life. After all, without the right amount of money to support yourself and your family it's nearly impossible to do everything that you want and that's what life is all about right? You want to be able to enjoy yourself as much as possible.

But in order to truly live a happy life you need to make sure that you are financially stable and that means saving money, getting your credit in good shape and eliminating debt.

Thanks again for downloading this book, I hope you enjoy it!

Chapter 1: Money

What is Money?

Money is the current instrument of exchange or mode of exchange in the form of coins or bills. It is a way for an individual to trade what he possesses for what he desires.

Myths about Money

There are various myths about money, for different people and cultures. Many people allow their beliefs about money control the way they spend, save and even the way they handle it.

When it comes to finances, many people believe they are doing as well as they possibly can. They may think they are accumulating savings, however they've never taken the time to sit down and figure out the math. They might be surprised if they did. Think about how these myths have influenced your spending in the past three months. Can you find any areas that need adjusting?

Here are some money saving myths many of people believe:

Savings accounts are the best way to save money

Holding money for crises in a savings account is a great thought. But then again, if you want to save money, an out-of-date savings account may not be the best route to take. Unfortunately, with the state of today's economy, low interests rates don't keep up with increasing inflation.

Savings accounts are still a good idea if you want to save, but keep in mind, there are other methods to saving that yield higher interest, increasing your finances in the long run.

Buying items on sale always saves money

Things may seem like they're a good price when they're on sat at 10%, 20% or even 30% off, but the reality is, you might not be saving any money. For some of us sale shopping is addicting, and instead of saving money, we spend unnecessarily. Often sale shopping results in spending twice as much as usual because we think we're saving and end up buying way too much. And, in the end we've overspent.

When shopping sales, it is better to buy what we really need and forego the things we simply want, especially when it's something that won't be used, worn or eaten.

*Tip: Combining coupons with sale prices, when possible, saves the most money. When done correctly can even get some items for free.

Refinancing your home saves on interest

Refinancing your home doesn't necessarily mean you will save very much in the long run. It is true that the monthly payment is reduced, however it increases the amount of time you'll be paying for the home. Another 30-year term after having paid for the first 10 years mean you'll be paying for 40 years instead of the original 30. If you calculate the current payment and the previous payments, you might find you aren't actually saving anything.

If saving money on the mortgage is what you want, the best course is to refinance for a reduced rate and a shorter term. Your monthly payment may not decrease, but your total repayment could.

0% interest credit cards save money

When you obtain a credit card that has an initial interest rate of 0% for a specified amount of time, you'll save on interest in the beginning. However, when the interest rate kicks in, it is usually higher than you bargained for at 20% to 30%. If you fail to repay the total balance at the end of the interest free period, you'll end up paying for the items you purchased on the card, and the high interest rates. These cards are costlier than they appear.

When applying for credit cards, keep in mind that a high limit and a lower interest rate or a lower limit and a low interest rate are the best options. Interest free periods are bait and switch tactics.

Savings depends on income

The amount of money you make does not make a difference or influence your saving capability. It is possible to save, even on a limited income. All you need to do is spend less than you earn, which is possible with budgeting. If you're spending money as soon as you make it, then it's impossible to save. As a matter of fact, you may possibly be spending a lot more than you bring in.

If you're waiting to make more money to begin saving, you may never start. Socking away even a dollar a day or a few dollars a week begins to add up.

 *Tip: Use an empty pickle or mayonnaise jar to store change. When it fills up, roll the coins and deposit them in your savings. You might be surprised what you end up with at the end of the year.

Chapter 2: Add Any Missing Accounts

In addition to disputing your incorrect or incomplete information on your credit report, you may want to ask your CRA to add information of any missing accounts that makes you look creditworthy.

Liz Weston, author of "Your Credit Score." says "If there's a known error on an account, and you can provide legitimate documentation showing it's an error, you can get a quick recalculation of your score to help with a lending decision,"

Information That Makes You Look Financially Stable:

• Present Employment -this includes your present employer's name and address along with your designation. The addition of your designation should be added only if you think it will make you look more financially capable. However, present employment information is a definite financial stability alert.

• Previous Employment - if your present job is lesser than two years, make sure that you add your previous employment along with your designation.

• Current Residence - if you own your residence, it's good if you can list it on your credit report. However, do not do this if you think a creditor can take it against you. Real estate can be an excellent source of information for creditors.

• Phone Number - if it is unlisted, it's a good idea if you can give it to your CRA. Creditors who cannot verify a phone number may be reluctant to give you credit. On the other hand, listing your phone number makes it easier for any creditor to directly contact you.

• Date Of Birth – Creditors would probably not grant you any credit if they cannot verify your age.

• Your Social Security number.

Creditors would always want to see evidence of stability in your life and if there is anything that is missing from your file, consider requesting your CRA to include the same. By including information that shows your financial stability, you are increasing your chances of boosting your credit score. Sometimes, adding missing information can drastically boost your credit score within a month.

3 Ways to Add Missing Accounts To Your Credit Report:

• Requesting the CRA directly - you could send a recent account statement along with copy of your canceled check that shows your payment history to the CRA. Ask them to add the information to your file. Although, there is no guarantee that the CRA may include accounts to your report, yet there are high chances.

• Request your Creditor - another possibility is to request your creditor directly to report your missing account information to the CRA. Creditors generally have contracts with CRAs that govern their relationship and they might get in your information.

• Alternative Source - another way that you can add your information to your credit file is through an alternative CRA. PRBC, for instance, tracks down your payments that are usually not listed on your credit report. These reports are usually designed to provide a record for those who have a bad credit history, but are now paying on time.

Chapter 3: It's (Mostly) All About The

Payments

The single biggest consideration when it comes to your credit score, regardless of who the credit-score generating agency is, is your ability to pay your obligations when they fall due. That's why if you want to increase your credit score and keep it that way, you must do all you can to make sure that you make your payments on time – even earlier if possible. Here are some of the payment-related things you can do to help boost your credit score.

Timely Payments

Given that your payment history comprises the biggest chunk of your credit score, late or missed payments comprises 35% of your credit score almost instantaneously! That's so easy to remember to the point of becoming a disadvantage.

How so? It's so easy that many people take it for granted, which results in missed or late payments. It's like that friend or family member you always take for granted because they're always there, i.e., easy to get hold of. That's why even though it's common sense not to miss payments or make late ones, we all need to be reminded about it.

You can leverage on today's available technologies to make sure that missing or making late payments on your financial obligations is practically impossible. First, you can sign up for an automatic payment scheme with your bank, this method it the most simple, and worth the time to set up. Because it's automated, amnesia's ability to rob you of the opportunity to pay your obligations on time will be completely neutralized. But that's assuming that your accounts have enough balance of course. But what if you don't have enough money to meet your upcoming obligations on a regular basis?

One of the best things you can do is to contact the institution to which you owe money. Ask their people if it's possible to adjust your due date to a later one, which can give you much needed space and time for timely payment.

What if your monthly budget is as tight as your skinny jeans after a buffet dinner on a day you fasted? That's an altogether whole new story right there. If you have enough good credit, why not try combining or consolidating all the money you owe into just one debt that has a lower interest rate. If that isn't possible, consider talking with your creditors and ask for a grace period or a lower interest rate. There's no harm in trying. If you succeed, you may be able to bring down the amount of your monthly financial obligations to the point where you can start paying them on time every month.

Your last option – if a lower interest rate just won't cut it for you – is to negotiate with your creditors for a restructuring of your existing obligations. By restructuring, I mean extending the number of months or years to pay off the amounts you owe without having to be levied with high interest and penalties or charges. It may be a long shot but there's no harm in trying and not trying can prove to be financially fatal for you.

Assuming you do have sufficient funds, make timely payments are always done. Whether you need the bank to remind you, or you use good old fashioned paper calendar.

Increase Your Payment Frequency

One of the biggest financial blunders you can commit in terms of payments in relation to your credit score is to think that you're all good for as long as you pay off your obligations – particularly your credit cards – as they fall due every month, even if you tend to max out your limits or always come close to maxing them out. Why's it a mistake? It's because financial institutions you borrowed money from only report your outstanding balances once every month. This practice leads to high reported monthly balances that can make credit-scoring agencies think that you're over utilizing your credit facilities. And that increases your perceived credit risk and ultimately, can lead to lower credit scores.

It may sound a bit complicated so bear with me for a moment and allow me to give an example. Let's say your credit card has a limit of $1,500 and even better, it's one that gives you rewards. As such, you tend to use it as much as you can, nearly maxing it out every month for the rewards. And every time the bill's due, you're able to pay it completely. To the untrained financial eye, that's a very good way to use credit cards. But for someone who knows a thing or two about credit scores, particularly credit utilization ratios, it's not something to do cartwheels over.

With the example given above, it will appear to the credit score-generating agency that you're regularly maxing out or are nearly maxing out your credit limit. Because they only take the numbers into consideration and don't have the time or resources to ask you why you're utilizing practically your whole credit limit, they'll take the numbers as they are and reasonably assume that your credit risk is high due to some financial challenges or inability to control spending. And you know how that can impact your credit score, right? Right?

A simple solution to this is to make smaller but more frequent payments throughout the month. For example, you can pay off your balance every week so that it'll appear that your running balances are much lower, which will be very beneficial for your credit score. So instead of paying everything at once when the bill's due, pay everything off every week or two. By doing that, you can have your rewards cake and eat them too!

Past Due Balances

Whenever you miss a payment, your account will inevitably be considered as past due. And when your accounts become more and more past due, your creditors will resort to more serious or extreme measures just to make sure your account becomes updated again in terms of payments.

If your accounts are just a wee bit past due, your creditors' collection efforts may not be much, i.e., you may only get a friendly reminder via a phone call, email or text message reminding you that you missed your payment and that you must make it as soon as possible. But if your account becomes more and more past due, i.e., the number of days it's already past due increases, the more serious the actions your creditors may resort to such as threats of legal action like foreclosures or court cases. And when it comes to your credit score, the longer your account has been past due, the lower your component score – and consequently, overall credit score – will be.

So if you have past due accounts, there are some things you can do to address this, which can boost your credit score and get it back on track. One is to pay off the whole past due balance immediately in one fell swoop. By doing this, you can almost instantaneously bring your account back into the land of the living and in the process, restore your credit score to its former glory. However, the bigger the amount of your past due balance, the bigger the minimum payments will be as interest and charges would've already been incorporated into the amount. But nevertheless, it's still the best and fastest way to prevent your account from totally dying – or being sent to the mortuary called collection agencies – and bringing your credit score along with it to the grave.

Another way you can handle your past due balances in order to bring your credit score back up is to just catch up on your payments. Let's face it, paying off the entire past due balance may be too difficult to do with just one lump sum payment. Reach out to your creditors and negotiate for you to be allowed to pay off your past due balances within 3 to 6 months, if needed. That way, you'll be able to gradually wipe out your past due balances.

If your creditors don't formally agree to a staggered payment of past due balances? Just add extra payments until you're able to completely catch up and reinstate your account's status as current. Just bear in mind that while you're still making your catch up payments, it'll still be considered past due. Your account will only be restored to its "current" status once you complete all your catch up payments, i.e., settle your past due balances in full. And if you're not able to catch up by the time your past due account turns 180 days old, it may be completely charged off by your creditors and damage your payment history and credit score.

Re-Age Your Past Due Account

If you can actually pay the whole amount of the past due balance without the interest and charges that bloat the amount to mutant proportions, it'd do you good to ask your creditor if it's possible to re-set or re-age your past due account. Why? Doing so can make your delinquencies vanish. While creditors aren't obliged to re-age past due accounts, some do agree to re-age such accounts particularly if it's a borrower's first time to become past due. There's no harm in asking so why not do so?

Debt Consolidation

When you consolidate your debts, especially the past due ones, you don't actually get to pay them off completely. What it does however, is to make them current again, easier to pay, and highly unlikely to be charged off, all of which are big boosts to your credit score.

Consolidating your debts means you retire the old ones and give birth to a new one. That's why I mentioned consolidation doesn't really help you pay off your past due debts completely in one fell swoop. But since you'll be effectively taking on new debt, it's crucial that before you consent to the consolidation, you've read the new debt's payment terms and conditions carefully and exhaustively. Doing so will help you minimize or eliminate risks of being surprised by subsequent increases in interest rate and payment amounts when a prescribed honeymoon period eventually comes to an end.

Negotiate and Settle

If all else fails and you estimate that it's practically unrealistic for you to become updated in your payments, you can go for broke and try to negotiate a possible settlement plan with your creditors. Such a settlement plan can be one in which the creditor agrees to you a smaller lump-sum payment that'll extinguish the whole debt. Usually, this involves negotiating for the cancellation of exorbitant interest and charges in order to help bring down the total amount owed and allow for the complete payment of the actual past due amount.

One caveat to this move: you must ensure that by the time you approach your creditors to negotiate for a smaller lump-sum payment, you actually have the money for making your proposed lump-sum payment. Most creditors are open to such a settlement because at the end of the day, they'd be happy just to get their money back with some reasonable amount of interest because they know that in many cases, insisting on what they believe is due to them leads to eventual debt write-offs. As such, you must neither abuse nor take for granted such good faith if you'd like to eventually settle your past due accounts and inject much needed life into your credit score.

Use Your Card To Pay Rent, Utilities, Etc.

When it comes to payment history, it's not just your delinquencies that matter. Credit scoring agencies or companies also look at your payment successes, i.e., the payments that you were able to make on time. It goes without saying that the more payments you make on a regular basis, the more you can establish your capacity to pay your obligations when they fall due, i.e. low credit risk. And since your credit score is all about measuring your credit risk, more successful payments mean a higher credit score.

Therefore, if you want to increase your successful payment history records, then use your card more often by paying for regularly occurring expenses that you are normally able to pay for on time using cash, such as rent and utilities. Pay them off every week or two – as mentioned earlier in this chapter – to help improve your credit score. Just make sure you don't "max out" regularly on your credit limit and keep your credit utilization ratio to acceptable limits, which we'll discuss in more detail in the next chapter.

Chapter 4: Work It Out

The first thing you need to do is figure out what's going on with your credit report. So take a moment and find your credit report. There are many ways that you can get a copy. Some websites will allow you to access it completely free while others will ask you for credit card information. Know that you are legally entitled to one free credit report per year from each of the three credit bureaus. That means if you contact the bureau they are required to send you a completely free copy.

If you don't trust any of the other websites to give you accurate information choose one bureau and get a copy to start with. You will want to sign up with a credit monitoring site (you can choose a paid one or a free one) later on when we get started in the section about keeping your credit looking good. For now you just need to have a copy of the full report so you can see what is currently reporting and whether it's currently helping you or hurting you. After all, there is good credit available too.

Once you get a copy of your report take a moment to read it over. Have a highlighter handy as you go through this step. The first section in most credit reports is going to be your personal information. Look over the information and make sure it's completely accurate. Is your name spelled properly? Is only the current and proper version of your name reporting? Are your current phone number, address and employer the only ones reporting? If anything on the first section of your credit report is wrong mark it with your highlighter and write what's incorrect about it.

The next section will likely be your closed accounts. Look over the accounts and make sure that you are checking for accurate information. If the account has any incorrect information at all make sure you highlight it. That means if the currently reporting balance is wrong, if the account number is wrong or anything else you want to mark it with your highlighter. Do the same thing with your open accounts. Pay particular attention to any late payments, repossessions, or cancelled cards and accounts. These are the things that are going to hurt you a lot more on your credit report and you want them gone.

Next, you'll find public accounts such as foreclosures, tax liens and judgments. Make sure you pay careful attention to these as well. These are going to stay on your credit report a lot longer than regular negative accounts and they also have a lot more impact as well. If anything is incorrect make sure that you mark it. You're going to come back to these marked sections later. Do the same thing with any collection accounts that are currently reporting. Remember any little thing that's incorrect on your report is important and should be marked.

Once you've gone through the entire report look at everything you've marked as being incorrect. Those are all things that you can dispute on your credit report. The reporting agency is required under the law to make sure that all information on your credit report is reported accurately at all times. If any information on your report is inaccurate they are required to remove it. What you may not know is that if they don't remove the incorrect information within 30 days of you requesting that it be done they actually have to remove the entire negative account from your credit report. This is a big benefit to you.

Now keep in mind as you look over your accounts that you're only going to want to dispute accounts that are negative. Usually there will be a key somewhere on the report that will tell you what symbols mean an account is negative. You'll also want to look for the words we mentioned, late payments, repossession, cancelled at credit grantors request, collection, etc. These words mean something is wrong about the account and it's hurting your credit score. Some even more than others. What you want to do is keep track of them so you can understand what you want to dispute when we get to that section in a little bit.

Chapter 5: Student Loans Explained

A student loan is designed to help students pay for university or trade school tuition, books, and living expenses. It may differ from other types of loans in that the interest rate may be substantially lower and the repayment schedule may be deferred while the student is still in school and then repay after the course are completed.

In the United States, there are two types of student loans: federal loans sponsored by the federal government and private student loans, which broadly includes state-affiliated nonprofits and institutional loans provided by institute and schools.

Federal student loans

Federal student loans are available through the Federal Perkins Loan Program or the Federal Direct Loan Program. Parents/guardians are able to borrow money at low interest rates directly from the federal government. Borrows should always explore federal loans before private student loans.

Federal Perkins Loans are low-interest loans that are available to undergraduate and graduate students with exceptional financial need. There is no interest charged while a student is in school at least half-time, and there is a 9-month grace period before repayment begins after the school ends. Federal Perkins Loans are not available at all schools. Please check with your school's financial aid office to see if they participate in the program.

Direct subsidized loans are loans determined by federal regulations for students with demonstrated financial needs. The direct subsidized loan has no interest charged while an undergraduate student is in school at least half-time and during deferment with a period when loans are postponed.

Unsubsidized federal loans are different from direct subsidized loans because they are not based on financial need. The school determines the amount you can borrow based on the cost of attendance along with other financial aid you receive. Interest is charged during all periods and will be capitalized. Capitalization is charged when you are in school and during grace witch a specified period after graduation before payments are required and deferment periods.

Direct PLUS Loans or **PLUS loans** can help pay for education expenses up to the cost of attendance but all other financial assistance will be deducted. These are unsubsidized federal loans for the parents of dependent students and for graduate/professional students who qualify. Interest is charged during all periods and will be capitalized so borrows should consider this factor.

Students need to explore scholarships, grants, and federal student loans to supplement savings before considering a private student loan.

Private Student Loans

Private student loans are credit based loans. Leaders will review your credit history, your ability and willingness to repay in order to qualify for the loan and your interest rate. Private loans offer different payment options that may include making payments while in school. This can help reduce your interest rate and overall loan cost.

Student loans must be repaid even if you do not graduate from school. Defaulting on a student loan can have a major impact your credit score and can affect your ability to get a car loan, a credit card, a mortgage, or even a job. These can lead to collection actions against you that can garish wages.

Federal vs. Private Student Loans

The federal government offer two programs through the Federal Perkins Loan Program and the Federal Direct Loan Program and some of the loans are available regardless of financial need. When students and parents/guardians are looking for loans they should consider federal loans before considering private student loans. The federal government can traditionally offer students loans at a competitive interest rate and come with entitlements, such as a range of payment options and benefits that private student loans are not required to provide. Federal loans can be "subsidized" or "unsubsidized." This means interest does not accrue on subsidized loans while the students are in school. Student loans may also be offered as part of a total financial aid package that may include grants, scholarships, and/or work study opportunities which can make school more affordable.

After you explored your options with federal student loans you can look at a private student loan as a secondary option; these loans are offered by banks, credit unions, and other private lenders. Private student loans are based on credit-worthiness so your credit history will be the biggest factor for the interest rates and the approval of these loans. Unlike federal student loans, private student loans many times have variable interest rates that can go up after consummation.

Federal Student Loans Are A Big Business

Federal student loans are less expensive than private student loans don't be fool the profits for the US government are well worth their risk. Prior to 2010, federal loans were also divided into direct loans funded by the federal government and private student loan which was called guaranteed loans, held by private lenders but guaranteed by the government. The federal government saw the profit of the guaranteed lending program and took over the industry by eliminating the guaranteed lending program in 2010. Now the federal student lending program generates billions of dollars in profit for the government because the interest payments exceed the borrowing costs, loan losses, and administrative costs for the US government.

The federal government losses on student loans are extremely low because the laws the US government put in place to collect on federal student loans are different from most other debts in America. Student loans cannot be discharged in bankruptcy unless repaying the loan would create an "undue hardship" for the student borrower and his or her dependents; this is unique because even IRS Tax debts are subject to bankruptcy. Most other debts there must be some kind of court process before wage garnishment but this is not the case with student loans.

Most college students in the United States qualify for federal student loans regardless of their income or parents' income and credit history. The only exemptions are students who have defaulted on federal student loans or have been convicted of drug offenses, and have not completed a rehabilitation program so this leave the door wide open for our young Americans to become trapped in debt before they receive their first job with this new modern slavery.

Chapter 6: How The Credit System Works

The credit system consists of three parties namely you, the creditors, and the credit bureaus.

*Creditors: These are the companies where you access credit from.

*Credit bureaus: These ones are responsible for collecting credit data from past and present creditors then compile reports, which are then modeled into credit profiles for every credit consumer. This credit report/profile is then sold to creditors to make different decisions including how much they will charge you for borrowing and how much penalties you should pay if you default.

If a creditor needs a report of credit consumers who have a specific credit score, they can then buy the credit profiles from the credit bureaus thus making it easy to target products and services appropriately. They (creditors) will send you enticing information on offers that you should buy.

Subprime credit data is actually the best selling for the different credit reporting agencies. This is why if you have subprime credit rating, you are likely to be getting countless email solicitations for you to apply to different credit cards. The reasoning for this is pretty straight forward; with subprime credit rating, you are definitely going to be charged more for accessing credit. This simply means that the lenders will make more money from you. If you have excellent credit rating, you are low risk and lenders charge you less for accessing credit, which means that they make less money when they advance your credit. As I mentioned, with bad credit, you might end up paying 2-3 times more than someone with good credit. In other terms, lenders will want to prey on you if you have bad credit because they are certain that they will make more money in the end. Even if you are to default, you are likely to have paid more money than someone who has good credit! Subprime data is such a hot selling product that the credit reporting agencies charge more for it; it is in high demand! This can be translated to mean that the creditors and credit bureaus don't care about you having good credit. In any case, if your credit rating is bad, they will charge you more! Do you know that over 90 percent of credit reports have been proven to have inaccurate, unverifiable, and erroneous entries?

Well, now you know why your credit score is always becoming bad even with all the efforts. These companies are in it for profit; they will even overlook when erroneous entries are posted in your report. In any case, they have convinced us to think that the reports are the gospel truth when they actually are nowhere close to that. So, in simple terms, these 2 players in the credit system can only be compelled by the law to put things in order; they have no interest in you having perfect credit because they all make more money if you have bad credit. This is where the credit repair process comes in.

The credit system takes into account both positive and negative information on your credit report. The negative factors such as late payments, overdrafts and the numerous credit accounts on your report all add up to reduce your credit score. Therefore, the less such items appear on your credit report, the better for your score.

Well, as you probably know, there is no indication on the credit report that your rating is good, bad, or average. So, how can you know what credit score is good, average (subprime) or bad? In the next section, I will show you the benchmarks that lenders use to determine whether your rating is good (perfect), average (subprime) or bad.

How good or bad is your credit rating?

Credit score could be anywhere between low 300 - mid 800. Let's take a look at the ranges just to give you a clear picture of where you lie.

720 and above

This is considered excellent. You get the best interest rates and repayment terms for loans.

680-719

This one is considered good

620-679

This is considered average (subprime)

580-619

This is considered poor. In this category, you get loans on lenders' terms and are likely to pay more for credit. You cannot afford auto financing if your score slips below this range.

500-579

This one is bad. Access to credit at this level is really costly. For instance, a 30-

year mortgage could have a rate of 3% higher.

Less than 500

Accessing credit with this score is pretty unaffordable. You might not even access any form of credit.

Basically, we all want a good credit score because this allows us to access credit at an affordable rate. As such, you should do everything in your power to improve your credit score if you start noticing inaccurate and unverifiable entries in your credit report. Let me explain this in greater detail to help you understand why you MUST take action immediately to correct your credit.

- Up to 93% of all credit reports have incorrect, unverifiable, and erroneous entries. This simply means that a very large proportion of credit reports need disputing because all these affect your score negatively. This percentage of questionable credit reports is so high that literally everyone should look into these incorrect, unverifiable, and erroneous entries. If you don't, you might probably learn the hard way; haven't you heard or read of horror stories of people who discovered that their score was ruined when they literally did nothing to make it bad. Many people only realize that their score is really bad when a loan application is turned down, which simply means that the credit score is really bad at this point. Don't just overlook any entry in your credit score because this could be the one ruining your score. Such things like the date of last activity on your account could even be enough to screw up your score. Creditors are notorious for changing minor items in credit reporting just to ruin your score and charge you more; they are in business, remember!

Don't just keep quiet when you notice different creditors reporting the same debt multiple times because this definitely makes you seem as if you are sinking further into debt. Additionally, don't just overlook the same creditor reporting the same debt in different account numbers.

- According to the law, creditors can keep your credit information/history for up to 7 years. However, it isn't uncommon for them to keep it for more than 10 years. What this means is that this information will constantly appear in your credit report, which means that it will be messing up your score year in year out.

So, how can you actually improve your credit score? Well, the truth is that this won't happen if you are busy sitting around expecting the creditors and credit bureaus to do something. You have to do something if you want to make your score better.

Well, the truth is that the process is pretty much complicated and frustrating to say the least. If you don't know how, you definitely will end up not having anything changed. That's why many of these companies are busy convincing people that they cannot repair their credit while they continue ruining our credit reports. Although you have the right to dispute, filing a successful dispute is a completely different thing. This book will help you master how to actually get things done in fixing your credit score. You have to ensure that you follow tried and tested strategies that actually work to get derogatory items removed permanently; you don't want everything to be restored within 60 days or more. The first thing you need to do is to know how to read your credit report so that you can identify any derogatory entries. To do this, you have to get up to date reports.

Chapter 7: How Credit Scoring Works

Understanding how credit scores work is the first step in maximizing or fixing damaged credit either with the help of a credit repair firm or on your own. First, you need to know that the higher your credit score the better whether you are looking for a new credit card, shopping for a mortgage or trying to buy a new or used vehicle. The higher your score the better risk you are considered when applying for any amount of credit. Knowing what goes into the calculation of your credit score and what can affect it either positively or negatively can help you make the proper moves to maximize your score at all times.

Here are some factors to help you understand how credit scores work. FICO (Fair Isaac Corporation) scores are a compilation of scores from the three credit reporting agencies Experian, TransUnion and Equifax. Each of the credit reporting companies has their own version based on different algorithms so the scores will vary. In addition not all companies that report their accounts report to all three agencies. Equifax has what is called a BEACON score, TransUnion has the EMPIRE score and Experian uses a combination FICO risk analysis score. Recently the three agencies have cooked up a combined score that very few people use called the VantageScore and are available from Experian's website. You can no longer get the real Experian score which can cause problems when getting a mortgage loan as you will no longer be able to maximize your middle score if Experian was your middle score.

Thirty-five percent (35%) of your credit score is based on how often you pay your bills on time. Another thirty percent (30%) is based on how much debt you have in relation to how much credit you have - in other words your debt to credit ratio. Fifteen percent (15%) is based on the length of your credit history. If you have several accounts open longer than ten years you will get more points than having several new accounts. Ten percent (10%) is based on your mix of credit - credit cards, mortgage, auto loan, revolving credit lines and installment credit lines. A good mix will give you more points as it shows you have a good sense of how to take care of your credit. New credit accounts for only ten percent (10%) of your score.

Some of the things in learning how credit scores work are what is left out when calculating your scores. Here is a list of what is not taken into account - your age, sex, or race. In addition how long you have been at your current job or how many jobs you have had is not looked at. Your income, marital status, number of children, or level of education are also not considered. You may wonder if the number of times you have been turned down for credit will affect your scores - it doesn't. Owning or renting your home, how long you have been at your current address or any criminal record is also not considered when calculating your credit scores.

Like it or not you are judged by a number and not your situation when it comes to getting a loan. Your credit score can make you or break you. It is no secret that having a good credit score will increase your chances of obtaining a new loan or credit card but many people do not realize this value until it is too late. It is time to learn how credit scores work.

There are quite a number of factors that come into play when figuring out a credit score. An end result is a number that can range between 300 and 850. This is on an increasing scale so the higher the number, the better credit rating you have.

It is possible to have a credit score of 850 but it is not easy. All payments have to be on time, all payments need to be for the full amounts, and how long it takes to pay off certain loans or debts is also considered. However, you do not need an 850 credit score just to have what is considered as "good credit". A credit score of about 650 to 700 and above is usually considered a good credit score. If you want to qualify for things such as prime rates on mortgage loans then you should shoot for about 680 and above.

When determining how credit scores work, we need to look at payment history, outstanding debts, inquiries, and the length of your credit history. The main factors are your outstanding debts and your payment history. These will weight heavily when determining your credit score. Before a lender decides to give you money they want to see if you are typically on time for your payments. The more often you are late, the less they want to lend you money. If your outstanding debts are very high, they might not want to lend you money for fear that you will not be able to pay all your debts back (mainly theirs).

Lenders depend on credit scores every day to decide whether or not a loan applicant should be approved. Using the credit score is an efficient way to make this decision due to the high volume of requests lenders receive each day. A simple query will let them know if you are a potentially good or bad client. While lenders may have other criteria for approving a loan, the credit score is a quick way to weed out those whose credit history is less than desirable.

If you find yourself in the latter category then you should start working on improving your credit score immediately. Since payment history plays a large role in calculating your credit score you should begin paying all current bills on time. The second largest piece is your outstanding debts. Get your own credit report for yourself and see how much money you owe to certain companies. Work on paying these off immediately. Call these companies and see if you can work out a deal where the payments are less per month. Some collectors will settle for a lesser amount if you pay in full. Knowing how credit scores work is the first step to having a more financially stable life.

Chapter 8: Thinking That Paying Bills On Time Gives You Great Credit

I think most everyone feels this way: "I'm sure I have great credit. I pay my bills on time and in full each month. I pay with cash for all my purchases." Assuming that paying your bills on time and in full or by using cash will guarantee a good credit score is probably the most insidious misconception of the credit scoring world. Many people just don't understand the rules of the game, and they end up damaging their scores instead of helping it.

The facts are that there a 22 criteria that go into determining a credit score. Most of which fall within five categories:

1) Your Payment History
2) Amount of Money You Owe
3) Length of Time You've Had the Credit
4) Type of Credit You Have
5) Number & Frequency of Credit Inquiries

While it is very important you pay your obligations on time, the credit scoring formulas look for specific balances that you should not exceed monthly. This is regardless of whether you pay your bills in full. This balance isn't ZERO either, and the creditor is unable to determine if you're completely paying off your bills each month. Actually, by paying offthe balance each month can hurt your score, because you're not maintaining the magical formula balance of 30% balance of the total credit limit.

Not Getting Your Credit Report Because it will Damage Your Credit Score

The facts of the matter concerning the number and frequency of credit inquiries that are incurred only accounts for 10% of your credit score. But contrary to popular belief, YOU will not hurt your credit score by making inquiries into YOUR OWN credit. You can pull your credit report every day for two months and your score will not be affected.

It is true though, that having too many LENDER inquiries will hurt your credit score. But how frequently you personally pull your credit report has no negative impact on your score. On your credit report it will show up as a "Soft Inquiry," and will not hurt your score. The Credit Bureaus are well aware that you need to and should be monitoring you credit. So they consider your pulling your credit report as being responsible behavior. Please do it regularly and often. You should pull your report every six months. The Fair Credit Reporting Act (FCRA) requires each of the nationwide consumer reporting companies (Equifax, Experian, and TransUnion) to provide you with a free copy of your credit report, at your request, once every 12 months, so take advantage of it. Remember to buy your FICO credit score from the place that gives you the same score as a lender will see. Go to www.myfico.com to purchase your credit report.

Applying for or having Joint Credit with your Spouse

Applying for or having joint credit is a bad strategy and a big mistake. Not just because of the possible issues created by a divorce, but also because married couples can strategically leverageeach other's credit. Just by planning ahead and maintaining separate credit their credit becomes a very important factor within financial matters.

If you look at establishing joint credit from a risk management perspective, you're exposing yourself to your spouse's behavior. This particularly can be an issue in the event of a divorce. From a strategic perspective, establishing separate credit can be a big boost to a couple's finances. If you are married and have maintained credit independently, you can leverage your spouse's credit when it becomes necessary. Take for instance, you need a line of credit but you have a high utilization rate (high balance) on a credit card, you can transfer a position of your balance to your spouse's credit cards. You now can walk into the bank or credit union with the loan application with a low personal debt and a higher than normal credit score. Basically, you can temporarily sacrifice your spouse's credit score so that you could obtain a better interest rate. This is just one way of leveraging your separate credit.

Not Checking for Errors on Your Credit Report

Would you believe that 80% of the people have an error of some form on their credit report? It's true, with 25% of those errors serious enough to cause them to be denied loans, mortgages and jobs. A recent Federal Reserve Board study of some 300,000 consumers' credit reports found 46% were missing at least one credit card limit. This error can severely harm an individual's credit score.

One of the biggest mistakes you can make is assuming your credit report is accurate. In all probability, you will have at least one mistake on your credit report. If you don't have one now, you probably will in the near future.

Not all errors are high priority; by immediately correcting them, you will greatly increase your credit score. Correcting errors can be very time consuming, but the payoff is well worth it. By prioritizing the errors by the impact on your credit score, you will be increasing your credit score the quickest way possible, as you correct them. Thus you can reap the benefits the fastest. Then attack the low priority ones, which have little or no effect on your score, but still need to be corrected.

High Priority errors can lower your credit score by 50-100 points. They are as follows:

☐ Collections Accounts
☐ Incorrect Credit Limits
☐ Incorrect Social Security # or Address
☐ Incorrect Bankruptcy debt discharged reporting

By having the right type and quantity of Credit Cards, while maintaining the correct debt balance to credit limit ratio monthly will increase your credit score significantly. Getting High Priority errors off your credit report will also make your credit score go up drastically. Even with a Bankruptcy on your credit report.

Chapter 9: Check Your Limits

"I am not sure whether I should pay off the high interest credit cards, the high debt to availability cards, the ones with the lowest balances, high balances, collections accounts, lawsuits, or just go shopping!!! Help!!!!! " – Evelyn C.

If you are wondering which cred

it account would be best to start with, I would say that you must first evaluate your goals and what you have available to contribute to cutting down your debt. You should consider that paying off installment loans, such as car, mortgage, and even student loans can benefit your credit score but not as drastically as paying off your revolving accounts, for example, department store and credit cards. Once you decide, there are different methods that you can adapt to paying off your debt.

Method #1 Attack the High Interest Rates

This method, which many experts suggest, is done by paying down your accounts with the highest interest rates. Attacking the account with the highest annual percentage rate with a medium to high balance will save you way more money attacking a low or medium balance on a low interest credit card. After one is paid off, they go for the debt with next highest interest rate, and so on and so forth. In some circumstances this might make sense, however I do not fully agree that this method is the most beneficial. For example, you have a credit card with $500 balance and a 19.99% APR and a $1000 balance on a card with a 14.9% APR. The smaller balance will accrue about $100 a year in interest while the account with higher balance at 14.9% will accrue $149 dollars a year. Here, it would make more sense to pay off the higher balance with the lower annual percentage rate because is it costing you more money in interest per year. This brings me to the next method.

Method #2 Attack the High Balance

As I stated earlier, one way to improve your score is by making sure that all of your credit accounts are below 35 percent, thus, if you have revolving credit accounts that are over 35 percent of the balance then this method may prove more beneficial to you. Experts say that for every $1,000 you have available, you should keep your balance below $350. Therefore, let's say you have four credit cards, and all of them having a $1,000 limit, one has a $600 balance, two have a $400 balance, and one has a $250 balance. With this method, you should pay on all of them, but apply the most to the first three cards to bring them under 35%. If you find yourself in this situation, this method might be best for you. Finally, and one that actually works best for me, is the method of attacking the lowest balances first.

Method #3 Debt Stack

When I am paying off credit cards, I like to do what is called the debt stack. I line up all of my revolving credit accounts from smallest to largest in terms of balance. I then tackle the smallest balance and move on to the next one on this list until I reach the account on the list with the highest balance. Now, I still pay on all of the other accounts ofcourse, however, I only pay the minimum and apply the most money to the first account I am attempting to pay off. Once I pay off that first credit account, I use the amount of payment I was making on the previous account toward the next one. This increases the payment of the next account, and causes it to be paid off much sooner than it would without the debt stacking method. This dramatically reduces both your payoff time frame and the total amount of interest you will pay on your debt. I have found that I do a better job of paying off my debt when I can see real results as soon as possible. As I said, this method is what works best for me, and in the end, we must all do what works best for our own unique situation, but it is nice to know what your options are.

Chapter 10: Understanding Credit Reports

The credit report contains your credit history. This is reported to the credit reporting agencies by the lenders whom you have borrowed the credit from. It is from this information your FICO scores are generated. So what exactly is in your credit report and how is it relevant?

Well, just like your body, to keep your credit as alluring as possible, you need to have annual checkups! Proactive checking and verifying your credit history can save you a lot of headaches when you actually need it. If you already know that you are going to apply for a loan, employment or want to buy a house, you should try to find out in advance which credit agency your lender will be using. With this knowledge, you can simply download that one agency's report rather than buying from all three available agencies. Reviewing your credit report will allow you to see if your credit is attractive enough for a loan to be granted to you.

Now, we know that your credit report contains a wealth of personal information about you: your name, address, Social Security number, and your birth date. It also provides information on your open credit accounts, including your credit limits and balances, and whether or not you pay them on time. If this is the first time you received your report, you might be confused! Don't sweat it. The information on your credit report is structured in such a way that is not immediately understandable by someone who is reading it for the first time.

One possible way you can tackle this situation is by seeking help! You might want to ask a trusted friend who understands this information to go through it with you. You can also ask the bank to assist you (note that this is a service and you might be charged a fee). You can also contact the agency that issued the report to you. Your credit agency is obliged to explain the report to you.

Of course, I would guess that one of the main reasons you want to review your credit report is for credit repairing purposes. If this is the case, you will need to know how to identify all the negative entries contained on the report! Here is a list of entries that may taint your credit report:

1) Bankruptcies (BK) – If you have ever filed for bankruptcy, the credit report will show the date you have filed your BK and the date it was closed. Some reports also list the amount of debt that was discharged in your BK.

2) Foreclosures/Repossessions – A foreclosure is essentially the same as repossession. A foreclosure means that your creditor will confiscate the property you used to secure a loan because you did not pay back in time. Usually, a foreclosure only applies to loans used to purchase real estate. Repossession is used to describe other kinds of property that is used to securing the loan such as a car.

3) Judgments – A judgment means a court listening. When a judgment appears on your credit report, it usually means that you have been sued in court and a monetary award was given to the person or entity that sued against you. This is very unfavorable for your credit history. Additionally, judgments are public records that easily find their way into your credit report.

4) Tax Liens – Tax liens, like judgments, are public records. They are usually issued by government agencies on your home if you owe state or federal taxes.

5) Late pays – If you are more than 30 days late on your credit payment, you will be reported as late to the credit agencies. However, if you are late for less than 30 days, you are still not considered as late for paying the bills. (If you have been regularly paying late but always settle the bill before the 30 day mark, you can breathe easy!)

6) Inquiries – Any requests by anyone (including yourself) to view or download a copy of your credit report is noted as an "inquiry" on your credit history. For example, if you borrow many loans in a short period of time, there will be an influx of "Inquiry" notes on your credit report. A high number of "inquiry" notes lowers your credit score because applying for lots of credit makes you a greater credit risk (even though this inference might not have valid grounds).

7) Profit and Loss Charge-Offs- These are generally used by credit card companies on debts that are considered as uncollectable. The big companies do not bother to spend time or fees to collect it. However, this are still considered debts which you owe and will appear on the credit report as that. It also does not guarantee that your creditor will not come after you in the future.

In general, these are some of the most common negative items that can appear in your credit report and they can stay in your credit report for up to seven years!

Besides understanding the blemishes in your report, it is also important to understand how to add positivity to your credit report. Here are 3 excellent ways to just that:

1) Seek Easy Credit – This is an easy way to build up a positive credit history. Many stores extend credit without extensive checks on the applicant's credit history. Examples of such stores include jewelry stores; furniture stores; credit unions; gas companies; and easy credit auto dealerships.

Of course, it is important to ensure that these companies report to the credit agencies, if not your efforts will be wasted.

2) Secured Credit Card – It is often a good idea to ask your local bank for a secured credit card. When you apply for a secured credit card, your past credit becomes less important. This is because you will be depositing money into the bank to secure the credit line. For example, by putting in

"X" amount of dollars into the account, you are able to charge up to "X" amount in your credit card. The important thing to take note of is that your card is not listed as secured with the credit agencies, if not you could actually end up damaging your credit.

3) Keep Active Accounts – Make sure that you keep your credit lines active after you received them. Of course, that is not to say that you should go around accumulating high amounts of debt, perhaps maintain a balance of $100 or so. When the bills come, you want to pay the minimum charges and pay them ON TIME (what the creditors look out for).

You need to display at least 12 months of good credit habits to be taken seriously so it is important to start right now!

Chapter 11: Do It Yourself Credit Building

Taking matters into your own hands

I mentioned a secured credit card earlier in the book. This is the best friend of someone who cannot otherwise get approved for a more traditional unsecured account. This type of credit card is called secured because the financial institution opening the account, usually a bank or credit union requires you to open some sort of savings account and deposit a minimum of $300-500 dollars. If you do not have that amount at one time, you can build the account up until you reach the desired threshold. The financial institution will then provide you with access to credit equal to the amount you have stored in the saving account. This is a credit card, not a debit or prepaid card, and it is reported to the credit bureaus as a revolving account just like any other credit card. Revolving accounts can make or break your credit score, because each month you have the chance to maintain a respectable credit utilization or a less desirable credit utilization. Credit utilization is the amount of available credit being used. For example, if you have a limit of $500, you use $400 of the balance, within the month, but pay $300 towards that balance prior to the date the creditor reports your balance to a credit bureau, your credit utilization will be $100 of $500 being used or 20%. The next month suppose your outstanding balance on that same credit card is $50, your credit utilization for that month is 10%. As a rule of thumb, you want your credit utilization rate on your revolving accounts to be no more than 33% each month. The optimum idea is to pay your revolving credit balance down to $0 each month, where possible to keep your credit utilization rate low and to avoid interest charges. Credit utilization is part of the formula that accounts for 30% of your score. Look at it this way, if you have a limit of $500 and an outstanding balance of $100 you have $400 available to you in credit you are not using, so the computer based credit scoring formula, views you as more qualified to borrow more money. So then, your score increases as you keep your credit utilization rate low month over month. Contrarily, if you have a limit of $500 and constantly are reported as owing $450, that makes you more of a risk for someone to loan you more money, because you are living off of credit, and this will lower your score month over month.

Another type of credit account is called an installment account. Examples are a car note, student loan, or mortgage. You may also open an installment loan account similar to the secured credit card to increase your score. The way this product works, your financial institution provides you with a loan, usually $1,000 and places the money into a savings account for you. Then you pay the loan back over a set number of months. Once paid in full, you gain access to the funds in the savings account, and gain valuable points helping increase your score to your desired number.

Installment accounts have a set payment each month and will have a $0 balance once all installment payments have been made. For example, if in order to pay off a car, you need to make 48 payments of $300, the debt will be paid off after 48 installment payments of $300 per month. Revolving accounts on the other hand may have a different payment amount each month depending on the outstanding balance.

Becoming an authorized user has its benefits

One thing I ran into quite often while working as a homeownership counselor is people with no credit history having a hard time securing a mortgage loan. The rapid way to appear to have credit history is to have someone add you to one of their accounts as an authorized user. Becoming an authorized user is a fairly risk free way to establish a credit history and begin building a positive payment record. Banks and credit card companies typically send the activity of shared accounts to all cardholders' credit reports. The primary cardholder can make this happen with a simply phone call. Once the account information finds its way onto your credit report, a history is developed. In some cases, it can add years of positive credit to your report. Proceed with caution on this approach. Make sure you understand how the account will be reported. Also find out if you are liable if the primary account holder happens miss a payment or go into default, etc. This will vary depending on the creditor and if you ultimately decide to make it a joint account.

The best approach may be to become an authorized user long enough to get the impact you need on your score, establishing or reestablishing yourself to then open your own accounts. You can then be removed from the accounts that you are not the primary card holder. In short, the authorized user strategy is common for parents who want to help their children build credit. If your parent has established positive credit history and healthy spending habits, you may want to request that they add you as an authorized user.

Framework for the art of managing debt and budgeting

The need for increased credit scores and financial literacy is not only a problem for low income families, but also for those who consider themselves middle class: One in four households earning between $56,113 and $91,356 have less than three months of expenses saved. While knowing how to strategically manipulate your credit score is one thing, having a solid hold on your personal finances is another. It is important that you begin today to establish an emergency savings.

This requires discipline and a definite purpose as in a reason why you believe having an emergency savings is important. If you are without the funds to establish an emergency savings today, its' up to you to be creative in how you add more income to your household. Knowledge is indeed power, but strategically applying knowledge in a way that allows you to reach a definite end is the only true power.

If you are one of the millions of Americans with a subpar credit rating, be honest about your debts. Take an inventory of your outstanding debts by adding up what you owe to all creditors. Start asking yourself tough questions about money to figure out why you have money problems. If you currently have credit cards, decide how many credit cards you really need. Consider consolidating credit card bills. You can do this by making a call to your creditors.

Paying down debt and paying off debt has to become an ongoing priority in your life for it to become real and for you to act accordingly. It begins with a thought, which will lead you to a definite goals with a clear starting and clear ending point. To help guide your process make or revise a family spending plan, and unapologetically stick to it during your set time period.

Start paying cash for everything you buy, where possible. Again, establish or maintain   savings.
 As for your bills, automate to be on time by using online banking and online bill pay. I know, some of us never know how much money is going to be in our accounts at any given time, but you need to begin establishing order in your finances, and it begins with being accountable. Having a set date for each bill to be paid through automated bill pay will help establish a new level of discipline you may not have experienced before. This may require you to reprioritize certain luxuries temporarily. Most importantly, you will be able to look to the future clearer. You have to be able to see and believe there is a day in your future where you will be out from under the hindrance of bad credit.

Chapter 12: What Does It All Mean

Credit scores can range anywhere from as low as 300 all the way up to 850 points. Where you fall on that spectrum can vary from one month to the next based on the information found in your report. Just like with your health, it is your responsibility to make sure that you take care of your credit and if you discover something is wrong, you must take steps to remedy it. To that end, you must know how to manage it properly. To be able to do that, you need to know just how the credit machine works.

You can Google credit repair services, and you'll probably find hundreds of them standing by, ready to take your money to help you get back on the right path. Unfortunately, many of these are scams and the few that are legit, are only telling you the most basic things to do. In many cases, these are things you can do yourself without outside help. Their main goal is to teach you how to fix the things that are wrong. What they don't do is help you to understand how credit really works and how to prevent yourself from falling into the bad credit trap again.

Understanding Your FICO Score

Almost every creditor will want to see your FICO score before he decides to give you credit. But knowing what the numbers really mean can make a huge difference in managing and taking back control of your financial future. As you gain more knowledge about how the system works, it can empower you. While other factors will weigh in the decision, anyone whose goal is to improve their creditworthiness needs to start with the FICO score as nearly all credit decisions will be based on it.

One of the first things you should understand is the scoring range so you can see what your number really means.

800+ is an exceptional score and is considered to be well above the average. Anyone in this range will find it very easy to get credit approval for just about anything they want. Sadly though, only about 1% of the population falls into this category.

740 – 799 is considered to be very good. While it is not the highest, it is still rated as above average. Anyone in this category will likely qualify for better interest rates and a wide range of credit privileges.

670 – 739 is considered to be good and is about average. They are not the optimum consumer, but they are considered to be in the "acceptable" range.

580 – 669 is considered a fair score. These consumers are usually below average and are labeled as subprime borrowers. This means that while they can get credit, it will be much more difficult for them; interest rates will be higher and they will often have to make higher payments for any purchases they make.

579 – 669 is considered to be a poor score. Consumers who fall in this range are often rejected outright in many places of business. However, they can get credit in altered forms. For example, they may be

able to obtain a secured credit card, or they may be required to place a deposit to obtain the approval they need.

This is just a basic guideline of how the FICO score is broken down. Taking into consideration your payment history, the amount of debt you owe, and the type of credit you have will help to determine what your score really is.

It is important to remember, that your credit score does not remain the same throughout your life. Every month, your creditors are submitting new data about your payment activities to the credit bureaus so your score will constantly need adjusting. Also, there are other factors that the Fair Isaac Corporation also factors into your score that may not be as obvious. For example, your income or how long you've been on your job will have little bearing on your credit profile. Also, those who have new credit or a limited history will usually score much lower on the scale than someone who has a longer history of credit to report. This means a low credit score does not necessarily result from missed payments or even being in debt over your heads. Sometimes, it is the result of something entirely out of your control.

In the account history section, which will probably be the most detailed of the entire report, you will find the bulk of the information on you. It will look something like this:

Creditor name: This could be the name of the merchant or creditor issuing the information.

Account number: This would be the identifying number of your account. In many cases, this information will be encrypted to protect your privacy and to prevent someone from gaining access to your account information.

Type of Account: This section will identify if it is a student loan, an auto loan, mortgage, or revolving account (like a credit card).

Responsibility: Indicates whether you are the only person on the account or if other users are authorized to use it.

Payment Record: Stipulates what the minimum required payment is on the account.

Date opened: The exact date the account was established.

Date reported: The last date the creditor submitted information to the credit bureau.

Balance: the total amount owed on the account.

Credit limit: What is the maximum amount of credit you can use.

High balance or high credit: The highest amount of credit you have used on the account.

Past due: Total amount of payments past due.

Payment status: Is the account current, past due, or is it a charge-off (meaning that you haven't paid in a long time and the company does not expect that you will ever pay them).

Payment history: Indicates how well you've been making payments since the account was opened.

Collection accounts: This would include any accounts listed that have been sent to a collection agency.

Credit Inquiries

The report will also keep a record of how many times there has been an inquiry into your credit. A lot of inquiries with no new credit issued will reflect very negatively on your score. It is an indication that you have been trying to get credit but have received many rejections, this can make a creditor seriously reconsider taking a chance with you.

There are two different types of credit inquiries you should know about. The first is the "soft" inquiry, which are those made by lenders looking for promotional purposes. Perhaps credit card companies looking for new customers. The second, "hard" inquiries are those creditors that you have actually applied to. Perhaps a bank for credit cards, a department store, or a gas company.

Public Records

The public records section is where you will find information about anything legal in relation to your credit. If you've had a past bankruptcy, any court judgments, tax liens, or anything else it should be included here. However, this is not for everything related to your legal life only things related to your credit. If you've had criminal arrests or convictions, these are not a part of your report unless they have to do with your credit (passing bad checks to pay on your account, for example).

Ideally, you want to make sure that this section of your report is completely clear. Anything in this area will have a major impact on your score and can potentially keep you from getting any type of credit.

The good news is that even if you have a bad report, the negative records do not remain there indefinitely. Most information will remain on your report for

7-10 years. Inquiries will remain for two years max. That means that in time, these negative conditions will eventually drop off and as long as you can maintain a good record, your credit score will naturally improve.

The Fair Isaacs Corporation is very tight-lipped about the exact formula on how they actually calculate the scores, but at least you have a general idea of what they are looking for and what parts of your report need to be boosted to improve your total score.

How to Read Your Report

When you first receive your report, it will probably be a little confusing. Now that you know what each section actually shows though, it will be easier to decipher exactly what it says about you. However, you'll probably want to first give more attention the second section, which will be a detailed description of your payment history.

First, look for any errors or inaccuracies that might have been reported. You would be surprised at just how many of those errors can be found in credit reports – insurance companies saying that the deductible wasn't paid, or that payments were late even when they weren't. Find those errors and mark them. These will be the first items you will address when you're trying to boost your score.

Once you have the errors marked, look for anything that might be fraudulent. Items for credit you don't actually have, for example. These could be a sign that your identity has been compromised and should issues you will want to deal with right away.

When you have all the negative aspects of your credit identified, then it is time to develop a plan of action that will help to improve your score.

Because we live in a world that is driven by technology and not actually reasoning people, mistakes occur all the time. False information in your report can bring about deep repercussions and will need to be taken care of immediately. It stands to reason that the sooner you find out these mistakes, the sooner you can do what is necessary to restore your good name and boost your credit score.

Your Credit Utilization Ratio

Finally, you want to look at your credit utilization ratio, which is your credit card balance compared to your actual credit limit. It is important to understand that this ratio will make up a significant part of your FICO score, second only to your payment history.

A high ratio indicates that you might actually be overspending and may be getting in over your head in debt. When creditors see this, they will automatically begin to think that you are a high risk of defaulting on your payments.

When you have a good credit utilization ratio, it can be very instrumental in establishing a good credit score and can actually help to balance out some of those negative aspects of your credit; at least until you start working on removing them.

Ideally, the lower your ratio, the better you look on paper. A ratio of 0% means that you are not using any of your available credit. A credit ratio of 30% or less is what creditors are looking for. Anything above that will cause your overall credit score to drop.

How to Lower Your Credit Utilization Ratio

As expected, your credit utilization ratio is constantly changing. Every time you pay your bill, your ratio goes down, and every time you use your credit, it will go up.

The best way to improve this score is to pay down your credit card debt. This is actually the fastest way to bring your percentage down. Pay as much as you can towards the total balance and avoid buying anything more until you are below the 30% ratio.

Another way you can lower your ratio is to ask your creditor to increase your limit. This may not be easy if you're already dealing with credit problems but the higher your credit limit, the lower your ratio; that is if you stop using the card until it is below that 30% threshold.

Understanding and being able to decipher the contents of your credit report is one of the most important things you can do to improve your credit score. Now, that you know exactly what to look for and you know precisely what needs fixing, it is important that you start working out a plan to boost your score and get you into a more favorable position with potential creditors. Over the next two chapters, we will discuss several things that can be done to help you to put a more positive twist on your credit.

Chapter 13: How To Increase Your Income

Easily

One of the best things about increasing your income is how much faster you can start increasing your credit score and meeting all of your financial goals. For those of you who think that it might be impossible to work any harder than you do, that might be true, but let's keep an open mind, shall we? We have already discussed how many of the items that Americans take for granted as being essential can not only be budget busters, but time wasters as well. Eliminating some unnecessary services such as cable TV or cutting back on the high-speed Internet or bundled services might leave you with a lot of free time on your hands. That free time could be spent on a hobby that earns no money, or on a more practical hobby or other means of generating additional income to help get you out of debt even faster. You may think you are constantly crunched for time and that you can barely relax as it is, but there are ways to put in some time and effort and then have your work pay off long-term.

Golf, for example, is an expensive hobby which usually ends up costing money, not making money. If you are a great golfer, however, have traveled the world playing at different courses, live near Las Vegas, where they have many fascinating courses, or used to go on an Irish or Scottish golfing holiday every year until times got tough, you could try to translate all that you know about these subjects into a series of guides that wealthy golf enthusiasts will pay for.

If you have discovered the joys of blogging but are not making any money at it, consider ways to start profiting from your blog. Then, once you are successful at doing so, you can teach the skill of successful blogging for profit to others.

Working online is one of the best ways we know of to make money from the comfort of your own home and set up your business in such a way that it will eventually start to run on autopilot. In other words, you set up your business once, and it can continue to earn for you around the clock, even while you are sleeping or doing other things, including working at your day job.

One of our marketing friends Tim Gorman was able to earn over $2 million in less than three years through his online article writing activities, and he was working from six-thirty every morning until eight-thirty at night as a U.S. Army captain. He never even created his own product to sell for years. He was making that money from Google AdSense advertising revenue. He spent three hours every night, and more time at weekends, because he was determined to give his family a better life and have a new career once he completed 20 years in the Army.

Life is too short to take on a second job that you dislike, but if you are developing expertise in your field or have a hobby that you love, you should be able to turn your interest into a money making opportunity. Again, even if you do not have any cash, or even a website, there are ways to make extra money online if you are willing to devote the time to it. There is affiliate marketing, in which you work for a commission on sales or on actions that visitors take to a website, such as entering their zip code. There is direct selling, such as Avon and Tupperware, or Pampered Chef. These will be more time consuming because they will involve face to face interaction with people.

The beauty of online marketing is that you do not have to deal with humans too often. If they buy from the companies you refer them to, those large companies will take care of any customer service issues that arise.

Just think, if you give up one activity that costs you money that we have discussed in this guide so far, and take up one that earns you money, you will be able to turn around your credit woes within three to six months. Or, if you want to keep a

hobby, or service like high-speed Internet, put it to work earning more money for you so that at least it will pay for itself, even if it does not turn a profit.
 One of the biggest advantages of starting your own small business can be the tax deductions. These can actually help pay for your hobby or interest as long as you keep the receipts, categorize them, and itemize them. For example, imagine that you love drinking wine and decide to start a blog about your tasting experiences. The cost of the wine can be deducted from any income from your blog. Then you would be able to make money from the blog in various ways, such as advertising with Google AdSense and other networks, or affiliate marketing for wine-related products.
 People who start their own business at home can take a variety of deductions, including money off on their rent or mortgage. For example, if you have a five-room apartment and one room is completely dedicated to your home office, you could claim a deduction of 20 percent

X 12 months on your taxes. The deduction can be taken if the "office" is used exclusively for work, so even if you do not have the luxury of a whole room, a corner of the den or family room or your bedroom that is used only for work can still rate a small percentage deduction. The kitchen table would not count, however, because it is not used exclusively for the business.
While you are hunting for the best ways to save money and earn more, you might also want to look at your taxes at your day job. In some cases, people are not having enough tax withheld and are getting hit with a big bill each April.
On the other hand, some people are having too much withheld and then getting a big refund. If you are trying to pay down debt as rapidly as possible, one strategy is to claim fewer or even no exemptions. Review your W-4 and change it as needed: http://www.irs.gov/pub/irs-pdf/fw4.pdf.
If you do this early in the new tax year, this will give you many months to pay

down your debt and then start saving for what you can expect will be a good-sized tax bill in the spring. The money you save on the interest on your credit cards should be more than enough to pay for your taxes in April of the next year, provided that you are disciplined and save money in your emergency account.

Even if for some terrible reason you might be a bit short, there are IRS payment plans, and any interest they charge will be far less than the APR on your credit cards. However, do not be too casual about this, as the IRS can impose stiff penalties as well as interest. Again, open an online savings account and set money aside from the additional money you will see in your paycheck every week once you make the adjustment, and use the rest for debt reduction. Then cut up or hide each card.

There might be a minimum tax at the end of the tax year for people earning over a certain income. However, for most of us, this is not the case. Also remember that as we have said, you can reduce your tax bill significantly if you keep all receipts and take appropriate deductions for various items, particularly if you start your own small business. TurboTax and similar programs can help you find a wide range of deductions that help you pay less tax. You can even deduct the cost of the program or tax preparation services by a professional from your taxes.

One of the biggest categories of expenses you should look at in detail, especially if you got into debt through no fault of your own, is your medical bills. The Internal Revenue states: "You may deduct only the amount by which your total medical care expenses for the year exceed 7.5 percent of your adjusted gross income. For years beginning after December 31, 2012, you may deduct only the amount by which your total medical expenses exceed 10 percent of your adjusted gross income. You figure the amount you are allowed to deduct on Form 1040, Schedule A."

Source: http://www.irs.gov/taxtopics/tc502.html

This page gives clear definitions of what is and is not considered a medical expense, but keep in mind that it can include car expenses and transportation to and from a treatment facility, supplies and more. As Jim always advises people seeking to improve their finances, it isn't how much you earn, but how much you KEEP. This refers to how much money you save, but it certainly also refers to how much tax you are paying.

Billionaire investor Warren Buffett only pays taxes in the single digits because he gets so many deductions. Using any spare time you have to better understand money, savings, taxation and investing can help you take the right steps to improve your credit score, plus start meeting your future financial goals, such as retirement, college for the children, and more.

Each person has their own financial goals, and there are many different strategies for achieving them, but as we have said, you can't start saving and investing wisely until you first pay down your high-interest debt. You can never start to regain the chance of great jobs and other opportunities, such as low-interest-rate mortgages, unless you are seen by decision-makers as less of a credit risk and more of a person who has taken charge of their finances. The only way to create this impression is to improve your credit score and then keep it high. With so many ways to save, and so many ways to earn additional money, you may feel as though you have three full-time jobs, not just one, and then need to find time for a personal life as well. It isn't easy, we know. If you wish to rebuild your credit, however, the short-term sacrifices can lead to long-term gains in the form of no debt, an emergency fund, savings accounts for all of the things that are important to you and your family, and even investments that can help you slowly and steadily accumulate wealth.

Action   Steps
1-Jot down some ideas for your own home based business or work you can do in your spare time. Also list any special skills or knowledge you may have that might be worth money from people who want to learn what you know.
2-Review your taxes for the past three

117

years.

Even if you genuinely have no free time to spare on freelance work or a business of your own, review your taxes and your spending patterns to determine if there are any deductions you might have missed. One of the best things about the tax preparation software is that it updates with the new regulations every year, but it is also not perfect, so check it over carefully. Be sure you understand the calculations that are being made. If you are not sure whether you have taken all the deductions you are entitled to, it might be worth it to go to a professional tax preparer. They can help you find deductions you might have missed and help you refile.

3-Adjust your deductions on your taxes as needed.

If you get a large refund every year, adjust your taxes so you have more money in your pocket each month, rather than have to wait until April each year to get it back. Find yourself owing taxes? Either make an adjustment, or budget for those taxes in

your overall budget.
4-Use any tax refund wisely, not wildly. If you are fortunate enough to get a refund, apply it towards paying down debts. Keep part of it in your emergency fund, but use the rest to decrease your balance on your highest interest card. The relief you feel when you have paid it off and will be able to start applying that money in a snowball payment to the next credit card you need to pay off will be worth any sacrifices you have to make.
Now that we have taken a 360-degree look at your life, expenses and ways to earn money and make your paycheck stretch as far as possible, it is time to start looking at other ways to strategically rebuild your credit to boost your credit score.

Chapter 14: Fraud And Identity Theft Prevention.

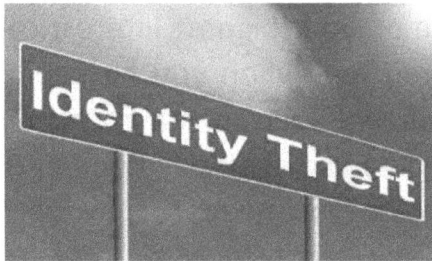

Once you have established a quality credit score, you need to do your best to protect it by taking extra steps to prevent identity theft and other types of fraud. The following tips will help you do so:

Respond to voicemail intelligently: If you receive a voicemail from someone claiming to be from your credit card company or bank, only respond by calling back the number that is printed on your card. This is the only number you can guarantee won't lead to a fraud scenario. The same goes for emails, even if they appear to be legitimate, you should only ever contact your bank or credit card company through obviously official channels that you instigate to ensure they are legitimate.

Take extra care with signatures: Not many people are aware, but you can actually sign your credit and debit cards with the phrase "see identification". While this will force you to show your ID much more frequently, it will also prevent anyone who is attempting to use it illegally from being able to do so. Unless they have a fake ID with your name and accurate signature they will be out of luck.

Be frugal with your credit card number: Ninety percent of the time any website that asks for your credit or debit card number "for identification purposes" has only dubious intentions in mind. Unless you are planning on buying something from the site you are going to want to avoid providing this information. The fewer places that your personal details are available online the less risk you run of falling victim to fraud.

Be diligent about your privacy: Even if you have already set them to the max settings, it is important to check both your browser and social media settings on a regular basis to ensure they are as you left them. You never know when an update could have come along and reset them or changed something else that affected them in some way. It only takes one slip to allow someone with malicious intent through, which is why it pays to stay vigilant. Likewise, every time you visit a secure website, take an extra moment to clear your browser's cache and history to prevent anyone from tracking down personal information that way.

Unsubscribe sparingly: If you receive an email newsletter and you aren't sure where it came from, never click the unsubscribe button. This will let the spammer know that they have a live email address and they will redouble their efforts, at best, or initiate additional tactics to procure your private data now that they have your email address, at worst. Even if the spammer has no ulterior motives than to get you to read their newsletter you are always better off just hitting the spam button and forgetting about it.

Be aware of online store security: When you are shopping online be sure to make a point of never entering sensitive information if the website isn't secure. You can determine if a site is using a secure connection if the web address starts with https or if it features a padlock icon in the top right corner. Either of these are an indicator that the website is encrypted which will make it much more difficult for fraud to occur based on the transaction. Entering your details via a standard http connection is little more than asking for trouble.

Have varying passwords: In addition to the obvious, such as not using birthdays or loved ones' names as passwords, it is important to have varying levels of password security for the most secure results.

You are going to want to have at least one password for low-security sites that you aren't terribly worried about being hacked, a more secure password for online stores and the like and a separate password entirely when it comes to banks or credit card websites that are more complicated still. You should never store your passwords anywhere on your computer or anywhere in real life where other people, with potentially malicious intent, are likely to have access to and, if you must write them down, don't keep them near your computer.

Cyber Threats & Privacy

Identity theft and hacking are growing at super exponential rates. It won't stop and will only get worse. The fact is that most Americans are already compromised and they don't even know it. It is estimated that over 80% of all residential households in American do not even have their WiFi router secured properly.

Wireless Card Scanners

These are hackers that will scan your credit card in your pocket at coffee shops or other unassuming public places. They have special devices or programs that can "see" the RF chips embedded in your credit card on their laptops. This happened to me once but since I was set up on banking text alerts I was able to stop it and get my money back. I now use radio frequency shield card slots and wallets to prevent this from happening again, which you can buy on Amazon.

Online Banking

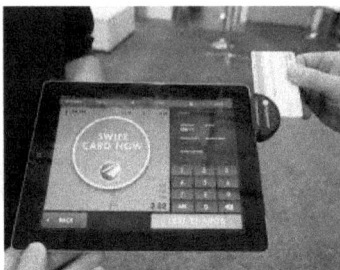

Make sure your network is secure and the browser is set to HTTPS when logging into your banking account. One small compromise and someone can steal your info, and ruin your credit. In fact any website you submit personal info on should start with HTTPS (Secure) URL.

In addition, over 80% of all U.S. homes do not secure their wifi router. Most people never change their factory default router login and password. Any hacker that scans your neighborhood (and yes they still do this) can generally determine what kind of router model you have from the SSID default broadcast, and then check to see if they can login using the default pass and username.

If a hacker is able to break into your home network, you can have some serious compromises. This often leads to cases of identity theft and fraud. Most often you will not know about it until well after the compromise has occurred and someone has used your information to steal money or your identity.

The cyber threats are VERY real and much worse than you think; they are only getting more complex everyday as hackers develop new technologies and methods to scan for weaknesses and infiltrate unassuming homes, people and businesses.

Shred your mail, bills or paperwork that may have sensitive personal info on them. You would be surprised to know that people still rummage through garbage to find data to sell or use for gain.

Use Secured Email

Almost everyone sends sensitive info via email and text not even thinking that someone can scan that data in "cyberspace" if they are looking for it. Since most people are now using Gmail,Yahoo Hotmail, **etc.** There aren't very many secure options for email if you are not using Thunderbird or Outlook. However, there is one company in Switzerland that has a service called ProtonMail.com.

It a browser email account with mobile phone apps that send and received encrypted mail and is very easy to use. They have a free account version and a paid account version, which is approximately $6 per month. If you send personal data via email such as tax returns, social security numbers, credit card numbers... Check out ProtonMail.com

Commercial Mailbox

Use a commercial mail box, such as the UPS store mail box, for receiving your postal mail instead of receiving it at home. UPS Stores are very flexible and can even forward your mail wherever you are. Many thieves still steal mail in an attempt to find social security numbers, checks, or anything they can use to extract money or credit from a victim

Conclusion: Credit Mistakes

When it comes to credit reports there is one thing that should be taken into consideration. What should be understood is that mistakes happen. These mistakes are not "mistakes" in the sense of some irresponsible action on the part of the consumer or anything of a similar nature.

Instead these mistakes are actually errors that appear on a credit report. The erroneous information on the credit report could be reported incorrectly, belong to some other person, or even be against the law.

The fact that these errors can occur is a reason why it is important for a person to check their credit report. According to the Federal Trade Commission 25% of Americans have at least one major error in their credit reports. These errors are causing the millions of people to have worse credit than they actually have, which means that they are paying more for things that they are supposed to pay. This causes the snowball effect where they incur more debts, higher fees, and even loss of financial opportunities all through no fault of their own. In short, credit mistakes are dangerous.

In order to avoid the path of financial danger a person should carefully look over their credit report to spot errors that could actually be hurting their credit. Thankfully many of the errors are easy to spot and can be reported in order to repair the damage done. The most common credit report errors fall under three categories: personal information errors, account related errors, and derogatory mark errors.

Derogatory marks are long lasting negative records on a credit report. These marks generally last for at least 7 years on a credit report and have a huge ability to hurt a person's credit. Bankruptcy, tax liens, collections, and foreclosures are examples of derogatory marks. Because of the severity of damage derogatory marks can cause errors of this sort are especially dangerous.

There are a few key things to look for when it comes to derogatory mark errors. One such error to be wary of is a collections account that has been paid off still remaining on the credit report as unpaid. This is an obvious error that is easy to dispute. There will be documentation showing that the account has been paid and contacting the creditor directly often leads to satisfactory results in getting the issue resolved.

Another common derogatory mark error is a paid tax lien that has remained on a credit report for more than 7 years after the last date of payment. While an unpaid tax lien may stay on a credit report indefinitely, there is simply no reason for a tax lien that has been paid to remain after 7 years. It is a black mark on a credit report that does not need to exist.

A discharged account displayed as an active balance is also a key error to keep an eye on. This is perhaps the most damaging of derogatory marks because it concerns bankruptcy. A person files for bankruptcy as a last resort in order to gain some relief from debt obligations.

The individual has entered into a legal process in an attempt to address overwhelming debt. Bankruptcy changes the accounts a person holds and the person no longer has the same active balances they had before filing for bankruptcy. Therefore, when a discharged account appears on a credit report as active what this does to a person's credit is damage it even further than is legally allowed. The bankrupt accounts are already in a special legal process to prevent further debts and that means it is close to impossible to actually have an active account with a balance.

These derogatory mark errors should be immediately disputed in order to prevent any further damage to one's credit. While all credit errors should be disputed, it is the derogatory marks that are the most damaging due to the sheer amount of time they remain on a credit report and the severity of the impact they can incur on an individual. A person that erroneously has an unpaid tax lien on their credit report could potentially be feeling the financial effect of that mistake for life simply because they didn't look at their credit report and dispute the mistake. The other common types of errors should not be discounted however.

Account related errors are mistakes that occur which are still damaging but not to the same severity as derogatory marks. These are errors tend to be simple fixes that take little effort to correct and probably only occur as an oversight.

An example of an account related error is a late payment that has remained on the credit report after 7 years. Generally, a credit report only lists negative information on an account for 7 years, after which it is removed from the credit report. It should be noted that the debt negative items cause still exist and still impact a person's credit. However, after the allotted time they can no longer incur more of an effect, in other words the 7-year mark is the ceiling for damage to a credit report. When a late payment remains on a credit report after this time that means it is still causing a negative impact on a person's credit. This should not appear on a credit report and should be disputed.

Another common account related error is one that is more the result of simple human error, however it could still have a negative impact if left undisputed. A loan or credit card listed on a credit report that does not belong to the individual is an error that happens on a regular basis. There could be any number of reasons for these to appear but usually it is the result of a person that had a simple mix-up while entering data. The worst-case scenario is actually a more frightening occurrence because the erroneous accounts could be the result of fraud or identity theft.

The first thing to do in either scenario is for the individual to report the false accounts directly to the credit bureau which lists the accounts. This can be done by mail, fax, email, or over the phone. It is quicker to do it by phone however disputing the account by mail provides a paper trail that can be used to support the claim that the person is actively trying to dispute the false accounts. Whichever method is chosen the following step should be to close the damaging account to prevent any future harm. Thankfully the process of fixing this error often proves successful and the fraudulent or erroneous account will be removed efficiently from the credit report.

The final category of credit mistakes is erroneous personal information. This category is the least damaging of mistakes but still has an effect on a person's credit. Like account related errors, these mistakes can often simply be attributed to human error. Thankfully personal information mistakes are the easiest to fix due to them not being directly related to financial actions.

The most common error when it comes to personal information is simply having the wrong name listed. This could be as harmless as spelling a person's name incorrectly or using an individual's maiden name after they've married. Another common error is a wrong mailing address listed on a credit report.

Perhaps a person with a similar name lived at the mistaken address and whomever is responsible for correcting that information simply overlooked it. This could also happen when a person's employer information is displayed inaccurately on a credit report, a person with a similar name may have been employed by the mistaken employer.

Generally, mistakes in personal information have little to no effect on an individual's credit score. Unless the error is related to something along the lines of fraud or identity theft then there is no reason to be worried. Simply reporting to the creditors the mistake in personal information is enough to fix the problem and no harm would be done to the person's credit.

When these mistakes are made they can be removed from a person's credit report. These items are also automatically removed after the regulatory 7 years have passed, generally. However, it is also possible to remove all negative items from a credit report. The process is not difficult and can go a long way towards improving a person's credit standing.

One of the most surprising and efficient ways to remove a negative item such as a late payment is to write a letter. Often called a goodwill letter or goodwill adjustment, a person can write (or call, although writing is better) to a creditor to get a late payment forgiven and thus removed from a credit report. This tends to work best if a person has a good history with the creditor as that makes them more likely to forgive the late payment as a one-time issue.

When contacting the creditor a few key things must be discussed with them for the best results. First of all, an explanation is owed to the creditor for the late payment. Telling the creditor the financial situation that led to the payment being late could generate some understanding and sympathy.

People are not perfect and unexpected events do occur, after all. Creditors are not machines but are institutions ran by people who can relate to what another person is going through.

What should also be discussed with the creditor is an explanation of the history with the creditor. A person that reminds the creditor that they have been in great standing with no issue can reinforce the fact that the late payment was not a regular occurrence. Requesting the removal of the negative mark should be made only after it has been established that there will be no repeat of late payments.

This tactic of writing the creditor to remove the late payment from a credit report is often more successful than people would imagine. Creditors are always willing to negotiate with people because they want their business. It should be noted that writing the creditor to request the removal of a late payment only works for those who are in good standing with the creditor. A person with a history of late payments is far less likely to get a sympathetic response as they have not shown that they are trust worthy. However even in that scenario it is still very likely that the creditor would be willing to negotiate a payment plan at the very least.

Regardless of the one's standing with a creditor it is always a helpful and beneficial plan to contact them. If a person is not able to remove the negative marks from their credit report then they are still going to be able to discuss options that will lead to positive impacts to a credit score in the future.

That is the biggest secret to getting negative items removed from a credit report, simply contacting the creditor. Many people are afraid of doing so because they feel that it would be difficult or they simply want to avoid the confrontation, but it cannot be stressed enough that a creditor is always willing to negotiate. Combining this with the fact that the passage of time can generally takes care of negative marks on a credit report and that leaves a clean credit report.

In conjunction with a person checking their credit report for mistakes and monitoring changes results in a credit report that will remain free of negative marks for as long as the individual continues to be responsible.

Credit mistakes are common, that much is clear. With the proper tools and understanding is far easier than people realize to fix these errors, especially since these errors are not the result of negligent or poor behavior on the part of the individual but rather that of the financial institutions, creditors, and bureaus. Mistakes happen, that much is unavoidable. What should be done to fix these mistakes, regardless of who is at fault, is swift and steady action on the part of the wronged person. There is simply no reason or benefit to walking around with a debt on a person's record that should not be there. Nor is there any reason to ignore their credit report and the mistakes listed on them. Vigilance is a requirement in order to make sure one's credit standing is as accurate as possible. Bureaus and other financial institutions are run by humans, not machines, so mistakes should be expected. Again, staying vigilant is the key.

Chapter 15: Where To Apply For Your

First Card

When it comes to applying, I would recommend first starting with your banking institution if you have one. Walk right into a branch and ask to talk with a banker about applying, they will be happy to sit down with you. But before signing anything, make sure you let them know your current credit situation, so you can both figure out a card to apply for that give you the best chance. One of the first cards I ever got was a "student" card that was a little more lenient as it was designed more for people with little credit history. Be selective though as every card you apply for will place an inquiry on your report. If approved great you are in the right direction for terrific credit. If declined, don't sweat it- in today's world companies are tighter than ever with lending. What is important is learning why you were declined. The company will not only be obligated to supply you with a free report upon request, but also the specific reasons as to why it was declined. Take these reasons into consideration and see if there is anything you could do to positively affect them before applying again. If there is nothing you can do to improve anymore, simply try applying with a different company. Even do research to find which companies are being the most lenient with their lending. Once again it is ideal to have three cards you are revolving balances on, but if you are new to credit some history may need to be attained before applying for more.

The first card arrives

You bend the envelope to feel that sweep plastic card on the inside. It has arrived, and soon following probably credit card fever. Credit card fever is when the plastic begins to turn into other things you want. It could be that new flat screen tv, or a shopping spree record at the local mall. Before you use the card even once, it is important to know what you are getting into. Key things to look for with any card are what your APR and limits are. APR is referring to the interest you will spend on any balance that carries over to the next month. Don't feel discouraged if you see a 30% APR staring back at you, because with discipline and the know-how it will go down over time. First thing is first, figure out what 40% is of the total limit. Whatever this calculates out to be; should be your goal for the balance on the card. So if it's a 500 limit, go spend 200 dollars on the card. From here it is merely a matter of not using the card until the balance has been paid off a bit. So wait for that bill next month and be prepared to make a payment. If possible even set up an auto payment through the credit card site. Feel free to pay more than the minimum payment, but do not pay off the whole balance. A balance that does not carry month to month does not exist in the eyes of your report, and will act as a card not getting used. Whether it's the minimum payment or double the amount, it will not affect your score directly.

When should you apply for another card?

This is a good question, and if you feel your credit is confident enough; you can apply immediately after getting approved for the first one. If you continue to do well with your first card, the company may decide to automatically raise your credit limit. This is a very good sign and means the company has deemed you less risky than previously. When your credit limit is increased automatically it does not put an inquiry on your report. If you have not applied for another card a good time is after receiving your first automatic limit increase. I would recommend following this formula until you at least have three cards, following the previous principles for putting debt on each.

Dealing with your credit card company

When dealing with your credit card company there will be moments where it feels like tug of war. Because after all, you want to keep from giving them money; and they want the opposite. When dealing with late or over limit fees give them a call and see if they can waive it. Most companies allow some fees to be waived, especially for first occurrences. If you feel the interest rate let them know, the worst they can do is say no. If you have been able to maintain a good relationship with the company, they will be more willing to work with you.

Chapter 16: Strategies That Will Boost Your Credit Score 100+ Points In 30 Days Or Less Without Utilizing Credit Repair

The strategies included in this chapter are aggressive and unconventional. However, there is nothing illegal about them, and you will be breaking no rules. A lot of the time, trying to boost your credit score with conventional means will take you much longer than a month. It could even you years to accomplish. The strategies here will help you boost your score inside a month and they will be very useful, especially if you are already in a desperate situation.

1: Rapid rescoring

This one is little known. For it to work, you must have ample proof that the negative items on your report are incorrect. However, if you get it to work, you can see results in as little as a few hours.

It is explained in depth here:

This tactic will be suitable for you if you are in the process of applying for a mortgage or any other loan type and because of your low credit score, are being denied credit or asked to pay unreasonable interest rates. You cannot initiate rapid rescoring on your own but a lender can do it on your behalf. It will work with credit bureaus by quickly removing incorrect information from your report.

2: Take out a loan for some major purchase

Ken Lin, the CEO of Credit Karma, says this, "If you are within your means and are in the right credit range, a mortgage or a car loan will be a good thing for your credit. Even though the initial hard inquiry you obtain from doing this will initially knock off a few credit score points, adding to your credit mix is important and it will have much more of an impact on your score than the initial point reduction, on account of the hard inquiry you put in place. Simply put, your points will go up far much more than they will go down.

3: Open a lot of new credit card accounts

When you obtain additional credit cards, you increase your total available credit. Seeing as your credit utilization or the percentage of available credit you spend is part of the score's make up, increasing your total available credit will help your credit score.

However, this one could backfire in the future if you lose your discipline and overspend anyway, or fail to use your new cards often enough and have your issuer close them.

4: Take out a small-sized loan that you do not need

This is the strategy of "forcing positive activity to your credit history." You may already have an idea how this works, but let us go over it anyway: You will out the small loan and pay it within 30 days. There will be some interest on top, but it will be too little to really rock your financial boat. For a few extra dollars, you will raise your score quickly. It also helps that installment loans add to your credit mix, which, you guessed it, boosts your score. This works twofold.

5: Use retirement accounts to pay off debts

With this one, our recommendation is that you only go this route if you are extremely desperate. If there is nothing else you can do, then you can use 401(k) funds to wipe off debt that is seriously dragging your score down. The score boost, especially if the debts are sizable, will be great and will happen quickly. However, you are placing your older years in jeopardy just by doing this, so avoid this tactic until you cannot avoid it anymore.

6: Pull the identity theft card

If you really are not responsible for causing the different damages on your credit report, then you can easily file a dispute on the basis that your identity has been stolen. As a rule, only use this strategy if your identity has actually been stolen. Don't just use it because your spouse, child or someone you know applied for credit in your name unless of course you don't mind them going to jail for that.

Here are some signs of identity theft:

Bouncing checks

Medical bills for some services that you didn't receive

Unexplained withdrawals from your bank account(s)

Unexpected or missing mails

IRS reporting more than one return that's filed in your name

Debt collectors calling for debts you know you didn't incur

Applications denied because of background check or bad credit

Declined debit or credit cards

Any unfamiliar activity in your credit report

You can learn how to repair your credit after identity theft here and here.

Chapter 17: Existing Lines Of Credit

I Kept Existing Lines of Credit Open

This may seem counterintuitive, but it's very important not to close credit card accounts or other revolving lines of credit that you don't use or may be behind on paying.

The length of one's credit history is a significant factor in determining how credit-worthy that person is according to the banks. In Chapter 2, I shared that the length of your credit history contributes to approximately 15% of your FICO score.

When I became serious about improving my credit, I closed several open lines of credit that I didn't need. In my mind, I was really trying to trim away everything I didn't use or need. I also didn't want to be tempted by my department store credit cards either. Closing these accounts was a big mistake and made my credit situation even worse. Not only did I have negative items on my credit report, but now because I closed accounts that I had for a long time, I inadvertently shortened my credit history. This is a mistake that's still affecting my credit score today – almost 12 years later.

The bottom line: Closing your existing accounts (which may have been opened a long time ago) shortens your credit history and lowers your credit utilization ratio or credit-limit-to-debt ratio, which we learned about in Chapter 3.

If one's credit history of open accounts is short, that person's FICO score will be lower than if the history of those open accounts was longer.

As soon as old accounts are being paid on time and being brought current, the credit report and FICO score will start reflecting a longer positive credit history. After a while, a long history of positive credit accounts will have been built up. Remember: Patience. This will take time.

Once again: Your credit utilization ratio or credit-limit-to-debt ratio is the percentage (ratio) of debt you have compared to the available credit you have. If you close your accounts, you are lowering your ratio by removing available credit and history.

Important: Banks can, and sometimes do, close accounts that they consider inactive, meaning accounts that haven't been used in a while. I don't want this to happen to me, because remember the idea is to keep these accounts open, ideally with a zero balance or very low balance, in order to build a long and positive credit history. If a bank closes one of my accounts, it could reverse the good work I've been working towards.

To keep my credit cards active, I make a very small purchase every few months with each of my credit cards. I'll buy a pack of gum or lunch one day or fill my gas tank – something relatively small and something I would have bought any way. This keeps my account open and the credit cards active.

And what do I do when the bill arrives? That's right! **Pay it off in full and on time.**

Chapter 18: The Dangerous Downside Of

Being Declined For Credit

In this chapter, you will see that there are many factors that determine your credit score, yet overall being declined for credit is the most dangerous...

The person that is in danger of being declined for credit is one who has not "thoroughly reviewed" their credit report and score before applying. I have seen those that have had high credit scores at the beginning of the year, end up with a much lower credit score three months later. You might ask, "How can someone's credit score go down so fast?" The truth is that your credit score will always go down faster than it will go up. The tricky thing is that even an excellent credit score doesn't mean that you will get an automatic approval. An underwriter or the person making the final credit decision doesn't approve people solely on credit scores, but the history and behaviors that are responsible for producing the score. So if you have a 700 credit score but you just got your bankruptcy discharged six months ago you will more than likely need to wait some more time before you will get a credit approval for most loans. In the case of mortgages, most underwriters review your credit score first, but they also look thoroughly through your credit profile, which in some cases go as far back as three years, in order to consider the following:

*Payment History

*Utilization – How much credit you are using

*Types of credit being used

*Length of credit history

*New credit

*Debt to Income Ratio

Before I dive into the downside of being declined, I first want to touch on the factor, "Debt to Income." This ratio is critical because some people think that just because they have a high credit score that they can get approved for any and everything. Not true! If you have an 800 credit score but your debt to income ratio is too high, then you will get declined for most loans.

Investopedia defines Debt to Income (DTI) as:

A personal finance measure that compares an individual's debt payment to his or her overall income. A debt-to-income ratio (DTI) is one way lenders (including mortgage lenders) measure an individual's ability to manage monthly payments and repay debts. DTI is calculated by dividing total recurring monthly debt by gross monthly income, which is a percentage. For example, John pays $1,000 each month for his mortgage, $500 for his car loan and $500 for the rest of his debts each month, so his total recurring monthly debt equals $2,000 ($1,000 +$500+$500). If John's gross monthly income is $6,000, his DTI would be $2,000 ÷ $6,000 = 0.33, or 33%.

So even though you have a great credit score, that three-digit number is still missing some vital information that can make or break the whole deal. The reality is – a high Debt-to-Income Ratio can counter a high Credit Score!!!

Many doctors have seen this principle first hand when they have tried to get a home or purchase some property. They ask, "I make over $100,000 a year, why can't I get approved for the loan, do you know who I am?" The problem is that they are not considering the negative things they are doing to their credit out of ignorance. Some examples that I have seen are:

*They are maxing out their credit cards to support their type of living at an even greater level…

Or

*They have co-signed with someone that knows they make over $100,000 a year and have asked them to help them out. Of course, they only ended up making the first payment because deep down they knew that as a doctor, they could afford to make the rest!!!

The above confirms that money is not a substitution for bad credit. You cannot think since I have a 400 credit score I will give you an extra $500 to make it all better again. The only alternative to a very low credit score is purchasing things with straight cash. However, you cannot pay TransUnion $1,000 to increase your score to 850.

With the above myths broken, I now want to start explaining how being declined for credit is dangerous. First, I want to begin by expounding on the term – Credit Inquiry.

Investopedia defines a Credit Inquiry as:

A transaction whereby a bank or other credit issuing institutions views an individual's credit report in connection with a loan or credit card application. The purpose of a credit inquiry is to evaluate an individual's likelihood to repay the money that is lent to them (known as creditworthiness)

I wanted to explain the ins and outs of inquiries because many might be asking the following questions:

*Are inquiries bad?

*Can inquiries affect your credit?

*How much do they affect your credit?

*How many inquiries are too much?

The answer to the above questions and many others is that an inquiry is a snapshot view, at a particular point in time, of your credit profile. In addition, there are two types of credit inquiries, Hard and Soft Pulls.

Soft Credit Pulls include:

*Background checks (seeking new employ ment or apartment)

*Credit Card solicitation for pre-approval offers

*Identity verification of an institution or bank

Hard Credit Pulls include:

*Applying for a mortgage

*Applying for a credit card or any other ty pe of loan

*Activation of cell phone contracts

Soft credit pulls will not affect your score, but hard credit pulls will. In addition, the Credit Bureaus look at your credit inquiries in a unique way. You may be thinking, I want to get a credit card, buy a car and starting looking to purchase my dream home all in the same month. From the Lender's vantage point, they may see it as you are trying hard to get new credit and may be borderline desperate. In the eyes of the credit industry, the word desperate has a negative connotation connected to it. New credit and credit inquiries make up 10% of the credit score. The more inquiries during a specified timeframe denote desperation, which translates into risk.

In doing extensive research, when it comes to credit inquiries there is a term called a "shopping window." With multiple credit changes, I came away with two shopping window timeframes, one for

"45 days" and the other for "14 days." I will always recommend the shorter of the two or the "14-day window" to make inquiries just to be on the safe side.

To go more in-depth as it pertains to shopping windows, a shopping window counts all similar credit inquiries during a particular period, as one inquiry. For example, if you apply for multiple credit cards within a 14-day period it will count as one inquiry. However, this only works for similar credit inquiry types. For instance, if you apply for a mortgage loan, an auto loan and a credit card within a 14-day window, this rule would not apply because there are multiple types of credit applied for.

Inevitably, I have found that the downside of being declined for credit means that many people will continue to apply and apply and apply for credit until they get someone to approve them. This strategy is very dangerous because the "Job Hunting" mindset of apply with as many companies as possible has, and will always, backfire as it pertains to credit.

Below are the components with percentages that make up the FICO Score:

*Payment History – 35%

*Utilization –
How much credit you are using – 30%

*Types of credit being used – 10%

*Length of credit history – 15%

*New credit – 10%

From the above chart, credit inquires would fall into the last category of "New Credit." In addition, there are two sub-factors that are also reviewed within this category which are:

*The number of inquiries within the last 1 2 months

*The number of trade lines opened in the l ast 12 months

Comparing these above factors reveal and confirm that the "Job Hunting" strategy will decrease your credit score very quickly. I always recommend that one doesn't apply for any more credit until you "thoroughly review" your credit report and score to determine what is the cause of the decline. In fact, the credit laws allow you to obtain a free credit report if declined, which gives you an opportunity to step back, before falling too far forward.

Points to remember:

*The truth is that your credit score will always go down faster than it will go up.

The reality is - A high Debt to Income Ratio **can counter a high** Credit Score!!!

In the next chapter, I will be giving you shocking evidence of the pros and cons of opting in and out of credit card and insurance offers. You will be discovering for yourself the "why" behind each offer sent...

Chapter 19: Keep It Manageable

Your credit limit is not a summit one sets out to reach, but a warning of the dangers ahead.

This summer my oldest son and I decided to build a vertical garden for our deck. We planted beans, peppers, tomatoes and herbs. And though it would be an enormous exaggeration to describe our results as bountiful, we were still richly rewarded. The reward came as we watched a word being defined before us: that word is "up."

There is an extraordinary drive for living things to climb, to grow, to strive, to seek higher ground. It is a deeply ingrained tendency. Most of the time it works to our benefit. However, in the realm of credit this drive can often lead to bad ends. At least partially to blame is:

the temptation of 'available credit'.

'Available credit' is a very friendly term. If I have $10,000 in available credit it's difficult to see that as a bad thing. The visions that spring to mind are of trips and cars and a life of luxury, albeit brief. Available credit feels like available cash, to be used for any purpose I desire. Of course, this is exactly what creditors want you to feel. But it is a huge mistake.

When we take this misinterpretation and add to it our desire to 'move up', our available credit becomes a powerful temptation; one to which we too often succumb. How easy is it to spend more than we intend because the funds are 'available' to us? How often are we shocked that the balance on our credit card bill is more than we had remembered?

Available credit presents a temptation that must be acknowledged and overcome if you want to avoid financial disaster.

There are many dangers to be wary of.

As your credit balances grow:

- you pay more in interest,
- you lose financial flexibility,
- you risk losing control of your payments

- you risk going over limit,
- your scores dive
- you leave little room for true emergencies.

Consider these two scenarios:

Scenario 1 – You use your card to make small purchases, keeping your maximum balance well below half of your limit, and you pay the balance off each month.

In this scenario you will pay little, if any, interest on your purchases. You maintain the flexibility to use the card in case something special comes up. The credit bureaus love you, and your scores reflect that.

Scenario 2 – You use 101% of your $5,000 limit and make only the minimum payment each month.

In this scenario you pay an over limit fee and your rate jumps to 24% (as an example). Continuing to make minimum payments, it takes you 15 years to pay off the debt even if you don't put another cent on the card. Over those 15 years you pay more than $8,000 in interest on a

$5,000 debt. Additionally, the account becomes useless as a financial tool and your credit scores crash.

Clearly, keeping your balances low and manageable is the smarter option.

But how low is manageable?

Everyone's optimal maximum balance is different, yet thankfully it's easy to determine. Answer these two questions:

1. What is 25% of your total credit limit?
2. What amount can you 'revolve' (pay off) each month?

The lesser of these two is your optimal maximum balance.

If, for example, you have a $10,000 limit, 25% of that is $2,500 (10,000 x 0.25). The credit bureaus typically reward anything under a 25% debt-to-limit ratio with improved scores, so keeping your maximum balance under $2,500 is an excellent strategy.

However, if you can only pay $1,500 toward your bill then that needs to be your target. Charging $2,500 to your card but only paying $1,500 leaves you with $1,000 immediately accruing interest and moving your balance in the wrong direction.

Additionally, if you are using multiple cards it is wise to divide your use proportionally among them. The credit bureaus don't care – they simply divide your total maximum usage by your aggregate credit limit to get a 'total debt to limit' ratio. However, by splitting it up you are less likely to push toward any one maximum limit.

But very savvy people who know all this still find themselves with balances that get out of hand. How do we overcome this instinctual tendency to overspend?

Create A New Frame

Understanding what 'keeping it manageable' means for you is simple enough to calculate. Holding yourself accountable to it is not so simple. As we already discovered, the term 'available credit' works against us, tempting us to use money that's not ours. We need to re-frame this concept.

Denounce the term 'available credit'!

It is a siren song that takes advantage of our upward desires and will very happily lead us to ruin. In its place insert the term '**potential indebtedness**'. Both terms are factually accurate, but 'potential indebtedness' serves as a warning and better acknowledges the long term consequences of excessive credit use.

Just as a plant seeks to grow upward, it's natural for us to push up and to want more. But when this tendency is allowed to manage our credit decisions the results are inevitably disastrous.

Take control of your credit use. Keep it manageable!

Recommendations to help you **Keep It Manageable:**

1. Calculate your optimal maximum balance. Stick to it.

2. Remember that 'available credit' is a temptation. Reframe the term as 'potential indebtedness' instead.

3. Split up usage between your cards to avoid maxing out any one of them.

4. Cultivate restraint.

Chapter 20: Setting Up A Budget

The best way to keep your credit in good shape is to live within your budget. So setting up a budget is very important.

A budget does not need to be difficult or complicated, you can use a notepad, a spreadsheet program (my favorite) or an accounting software.

There should be two major parts of your budget, the income, and the expenses.

Income – The income portion should be set up just like your paycheck is set up. It should show your gross income and all of the different deductions from your paycheck. The reason we do this is so that we can easily see where our money is going before we get it.

Example posting of Income

Gross Income	Monthly	1,850.00
Less	Federal tax withhold	- 175.50
	State tax withhold	- 112.75
	Social Security tax	- 115.62
	401K deduction	- 80.00
	medical insurance	- 145.00
	other deductions	- 0.00
Total Deductions		- 628.87
Net Monthly Income		1,221.13

It is important to know where your income is going before it gets to your pocket because not all of the items are mandatory and even those that are, can sometimes be adjusted. In the prior example, if we needed more money for bills we could cancel our 401K deduction (it would give us an extra $ 80 a month to pay our bills). Another possibility would be to reduce the amount is taken out for federal and state taxes (but consult your tax professional first).

Expenses- On the expense portion I include several sections:

1) Large expenses – such as rent, car payment, utilities, food, gas, insurance, car registration (prorated)

2) other required monthly expenses – such as credit cards

3) nonessential expenses – We may each have a different distinction for what is nonessential but at the beginning all expenses that do not fit into one of the other two areas should be placed here.

Example Posting of expenses

Rent	$ 850
Car payment	275
Electric Bill	95
Food	350
Car Insurance	180
Visa card # 1	25
Visa card # 2	30
Starbucks	120
Bowling	75
Movies	70

The amounts on some of the expense categories may change monthly, for example, how much you spend at Starbucks™ will not be the same month to month, same with the gas, food, and other expenses. **It is important to keep a record of these types of expenses on a daily basis**. You can keep the receipts and record them later or do as my daughter does and write the expense into a journal when you pay for the expense. You will be surprised how much you spend on a daily basis.

Once you compare your net monthly income to your monthly expenses you can determine whether everything is okay or whether you need to make a change. If you need a change, it may be to increase your take-home pay, reduce your expenses or a combination of the two.

Increasing your take-home income comes down to either increasing your income by working more hours, getting a better paying job, etc. or by reducing the deductions taken out of your paycheck. Look at voluntary deductions such as 401K plans, voluntary savings accounts, etc. Do you need them at this time? A 401K plan is a great thing to have as long as you can afford to eat and have a place to live. But if it is a choice between putting gas in the car and putting money away for retirement, I would put gas in the car. I can always start saving later for retirement. Another thing to look at is to find out what your tax returns will look like at the end of the year. For example, if you are a single person and your total income for the year will be $8,000 then the question is whether you will have any "taxable income" for the year. If you will not have any "taxable income" then there is no reason to have any money withheld, from your paycheck, for federal or state taxes. You can use that money now. How do you find out what your "taxable income" will be for the entire year? You can ask a tax professional or use last year's tax forms with this year's numbers (it won't be exact but pretty close).

Reducing your expenses will also be easier once you can see exactly where your money is going. Start by looking at the big expenses and thinking about whether they can be reduced. You should be shopping for car insurance every two years. Your driving record and experience is changing all the time. You may be able to get cheaper rates from a different insurance company. Look to see if there are any deals available for your telephone, cable, Wi-Fi services in your area. Could you switch to store brand food instead of national brands?

Maybe buy gasoline from a cheaper brand? Could you reduce the interest rate on your credit cards? I rarely pay more than 3% interest rate on my credit cards; I'll explain how you can do this in Chapter 9. Can you get a roommate?

On the nonessential expenses, try and get more specific as to their classification and which ones you can live without (or at least with less of). Are they truly nonessentials to you? Can you live with going to Starbucks™ once a week instead of every day? Could you rent movies from Redbox™ instead of going to the movies every weekend?

It is said that a problem cannot be fixed until it is identified. Putting your expenses down on paper will help you live better. Setting up a budget for the future requires knowing if you have any money left over after paying all the mandatory bills. Write down how much you think you should spend, as a maximum, on nonessential expenses. Complete a separate list for each month and compare your progress each month. Most of us don't make huge changes quickly, the reminder of what you are doing and where you want to be will help get you there.

Example of a budget

Income		
	Gross Monthly Income	$ 2,350.00
	Federal Tax Deduction	- 245.00
	State Tax Deduction	- 108.00
	Soc. Security Deduction	- 146.88
	401K Deduction	-

		100.00
Net Income		$ 1,750.12
Expenses		
	Rent	-850.00
	Electricity	-55.00
	Gas (for home)	-42.50
	Water bill	-30.00
	Cable TV/WIFI	-105.00
	Car payment	-145.00
	Car Insurance	-98.50
	Groceries (target $ 250)	-275.00
	Gar for car (target $75)	-100.00
(bal is $ 2250 at 21.99%)	Credit card A	-25.00
(bal is	Credit card B	-50.00

$1397 at 15.99%)

Non-Essentials	Coffee shop (target $ 35)	-85.00
	Movies (target $ 50)	-115.00
	Eating out (target $ 75)	-175.00
Total Expenses		-2,131.00
Net Income	(1750.12 – 2131.00)	-380.88

Based on this example, I need to reduce my expenses quickly and reaching my target budget will not be enough. I may need to increase my take-home income.

Chapter 21: General Good Financial Habits Build Good Credit Scores

Your credit score in some ways is meant to be a snapshot of your overall financial habits - especially your habits surrounding debts and other financial responsibilities. Developing some good financial habits can help your credit score by putting you in a good financial position.

Good financial habits will ensure that you don't get into too much debt and that you are able to meet your financial duties easily. There are a few financial habits that are especially creditfriendly:

Tip #40: Learn to budget One of the biggest reasons that people develop poor credit is overspending. In many cases, this overspending is caused by a lack of budget. A budget can tell you how much you should be spending on each item in your life. This allows your financial life to stay nicely organized.

182

Contrary to popular belief, a budget does not have to be constricting or boring or complicated. Simply note how much you earn each month, and on a piece of paper, write down how much you really need to spend on savings, rent, utilities, food, personal care, transportation, spending money, entertainment, hobbies, education, and other items. Make sure that you account for every expense.

Then, simply commit yourself to spending that particular amount on each item on your list. Of course, some expenses on your list will change each month - you may spend more on heating bills in the winter than in the summer, for example - but estimating can help ensure that you can meet all your financial responsibilities.

Tip #41: Live within your means Many people believe that if they only had more money, they would not have to worry about credit. In fact, this is not true. Many people who have money - or at least have all the trappings of money, including cars and nice homes - in fact have terrible credit.

The secret of this is that it is not your income that decides whether you are a good credit risk or a bad one but rather how you handle money. You could be earning $7 per hour and still paying your bills and meeting your financial responsibilities - in which case you will have terrific credit.

You could also be earning $300 000 a year and be in terrible debt and financial shape due to unpaid bills and excessive debt. The best way to ensure that you have a good credit rating - no matter what your income - is to spend less than you earn. That means living below your means. If you have a very small income, you may need to live with roommates in order to keep costs down. If you have a medium-sized income, that may mean saving more and entertaining less.

You may be interested to note that your income is not a factor in determining your credit score. Although your past and current employers are listed on your credit report - and although lenders may be able to guess your financial status from your loan amounts - your income does not count.

This means that if you won the lottery today or suddenly inherited a large sum, your credit score would not increase. With your credit rating, what matters is how you manage your money, not how much you make.

Tip #42: Get out of the spending habit We are surrounded with advertisements that tell us to buy, buy, buy. When we want to read a book, we buy it. When we want to go somewhere, we take a cab or drive rather than walking.

Stopping spending consciously can be hard, but heading to your local library, walking instead of taking a car, buying a used computer instead of a new one - all can help you spend less and save more. There are several ways you can save money and pay off your debts faster by spending less:

1) When you head out, carry a small amount of cash with you and leave your credit cards at home. That way, you will not be able to overspend.

2) Stop catalogs from arriving at your house or discard them unread - advertisements and catalogues encourage you to spend and buy when you don't need to.

3) Do it yourself. Eat in rather than dining out. Dining at restaurants or getting food delivered is always more expensive than doing your own cooking. Also, do your own taxes rather than farming the job out to someone else. Wash your own car, run your own errands, mow your own lawn. When you do something yourself, you spend less.

4) Watch less television. It sounds strange, but television can make you overspend - television contains many professionally-created advertisements pushing us to spend and spend. These ads are so well done that not spending after watching them is sometimes very difficult

(just what advertisers want!). Switching off your television can help you avoid temptation.

5) Make do or do without. While you are repairing your credit, channel all your extra money into paying off debts and reestablishing good credit. Make so with what you have and avoid shopping as much as possible.

6) Buy discount or used. Whether it is furniture or shoes, you can save money by refusing to pay retail price.

Saving your money by spending less can let you pay off your debts faster, something that can improve your credit score dramatically.

Tip #43: Save One of the best ways to ensure that your credit rating stays good is to save money each month. Whether you are able to save $25 a month or $200 or even more, saving and investing your savings will prepare you for financial emergencies, will get you out of overspending, and will allow you to build investments that can help you in later years.

With savings at your bank, you don't have to worry that sudden illness will make you unable to pay your bills, resulting in dings on your credit.

Saving ten percent of your income is a nice, reasonable goal. You can use your invested savings to make certain that your debts never get overwhelming. Most employers and banks will even deduct a certain amount of money from your paycheck or account each month to be put into investments.

This can be a very convenient way to save, as you are unlikely to miss or spend money you have taken out before you can get your hands on it.

Tip #44: Keep track of your money Most people are surprised by how quickly their money seems to be spent. This is because impulse spending and small-change spending really adds up. Small-change spending is small spending we do without even thinking about it - buying a coffee or a newspaper we don't need.

Impulse spending refers to simply buying things we don't use or need. In both cases, we end up spending too much unnecessarily, and this is a problem in credit repair because you want to be channeling as much money as you can into savings and debt repayment so that you can repair your credit.

For a month, try keeping a daily record of every penny you spend - including the money you spend on phones, the money you spend on tips, everything. You will be amazed where your money goes. Keeping track of your money this way does two things:

1) It automatically cuts down on spending. If you have to write down where you spend your money, you will be much more careful what you spend your money on.

2) It allows you to see where you waste your money and take steps to stop the bad habit. If you notice that you always buy the newspaper on Saturday but never read

it, for example, you can stop buying the paper on that day. Small savings can add up over the years and can put you in good financial shape which will be reflected in your credit risk rating.

Tip #45: Take out one pleasure and save it up

-Do you have cable? -Do you subscribe to lots of magazines? -Do you build your DVD collection so fast that you can't even watch all the movies you collect?

We all entertain ourselves with money, but most of us have at least one or two entertainments that we have either outgrown or don't enjoy as much as we once did. Cutting that expense out and investing the savings can put us well on our way to saving for retirement or paying off our bills. If you give up your cable television, for example, you can pay off your credit cards that much faster, improving your credit score.

Tip #46: Build assets and capital Whether it is buying a car, a home, or creating an investment portfolio, having assets can help improve your credit score by allowing you take out secured credit, or credit in which your assets are used as collateral.

When you take out secured credit (such as a mortgage) you enjoy lower interest rates and easier approval. As you repay your secured debt, your credit score will improve. Even better, lenders do look at the types of credit you have. If you have a mix of secured and unsecured credit, you will enjoy better risk rating scores as it will indicate that you have the means to repay your debts.

Building assets and capital is also a way of building financial stability which can help protect your credit score. If you have assets such as savings or investments, then you have a way of generating income or repaying debts in case of an emergency. You also have ready money you can use in case of unexpected medical bills or other problems.

Tip #47: Find more ways to income While you are repairing your credit, you will want to channel as much money as you can into savings and debt repayment. For this, having a second income or even just a few hundred dollars a month more can mean that you get your credit into shape faster.

Having a secondary form of income can also keep your credit safe - if you lose your job, you can use the money you make from a secondary source to repay your bills until you find another form of employment.

There are many ways to get more income:

-You can ask your employer for a raise. -You can start to sell something through the Internet or through a company. -You can establish your own small business that can be tended to on the side. -You can rent out part of your home to make some extra money. -You can get a part-time or weekend job.

Whatever you do, finding an alternate source of income can help your credit immensely.

Tip #48: Prepare for financial emergencies Few of us think about what would happen if we lost our jobs or suddenly became too ill to work. The thought is simply too terrible to contemplate in many cases, especially if we are living paycheck to paycheck with a job as it is.

The fact is, though, that financial emergencies happen to almost everyone at some point and they can have devastating impact in your credit. In fact, most people who declare bankruptcy do so because of a huge financial disaster such as sudden unemployment, huge medical bills, a lawsuit, or divorce. Despite this, few people plan for these problems, even though they can happen to anyone.

If you want to keep your credit score in good trim, you should know exactly what you would do in case of an emergency. Developing an actual written plan can help you by letting you take action to save your credit as soon as an emergency occurs. Some items that could be on your financial emergency plan could include:

1) A list of all assets you could liquidate if you had to.

2) A list of all extras or luxuries you could cut out of your life right away if there was a problem (i.e. newspaper subscriptions, cable television, water delivery service, Friday nights at the movies).

3) A list of any resources you have that could help you in case of an emergency. Maybe you know a lawyer who deals in financial facets of the law. Maybe you have insurance that could help you. Maybe your employer offers a severance package. Whatever it is, write it down. Keeping a list of these resources will make them easier to access in case of an emergency.

4) Other ways you could get money if you had to - jobs you could take, things you could rent out to others.

Tip #49: Get overdraft protection, insurance on your credit cards, or other services to keep your credit in good shape Talk to your bank and lenders about services they offer to keep you safe. Overdraft protection, for example, is a basic service that often costs nothing or very little extra but which protects you in case you withdraw too much money from your bank account.

With overdraft protection, you do not get a "ding" on your credit report or a charge for insufficient funds. In most cases, you get a day or two to add more money to the account to cover the gap. Some credit cards and other loans offer a similar service or offer insurance which protects you in case you lose your job and are unable to pay for a few months.

Tip #50: Get insurance Insurance for health, your car, your home, and for liability can help you avoid the huge legal and medical bills that can occur from an accident or sudden problem. For a small monthly fee, you are covered against unexpected events that can drain your finances and leave you with out-of control debt.

Tip #51: Get a prenuptial agreement and have a lawyer go over all your business contracts Most bankruptcies are caused by the fallout that occurs as a result of business failures, law suits, health costs, and divorces. Getting a prenuptial agreement helps to ensure that a divorce will not adversely affect your finances and lead to a ruined credit rating (keeping accounts separate while married is also a good idea, as your spouse's own financial troubles can all too easily become your own). Having a lawyers look over contracts can at least reduce the risks of unfavorable agreements that can put you at a disadvantage in business.

Chapter 22: Learning The Credit Score

Scale

So far, this book has relayed information to you on what exactly your credit score is and how you can maximize the usefulness of a great credit score in your life. This chapter, instead of focusing on more ways in which you can improve your credit (we've already addressed all of those), will discuss the various credit ranges and what they mean. If you already know what your credit score currently is, that's great. If you don't, consider finding out your score before reading this chapter. After recognizing how the credit card ranges work as a whole, the specific numbers involved will be analyzed in hopes of gaining more understanding.

Each Lender is Different

The first factor to understand before diving into the specifics of the numbers involved in credit card scoring is to realize that each and every lender has its own credit scoring system. Unlike other standardized financial processes like currency or income tax, credit score criteria will differ from lender-to-lender and industry-to-industry. It's important to remember that while the FICO system as a whole works to keep individual consumer credit as transparent as possible, the scoring ranges themselves were vary. For example, some companies have a range that starts at 300, while others have systems that begin at 350. Other companies might only have a range from 300 to 800, and a different company within the same industry will have a credit score range from 350 to 950. Knowing this information will help you anticipate how the way in which you are treated by potential lenders might not be consistent. The more often you work with lenders, the easier it will be to recognize policies that work to your benefit, and those that seek to make financing harder for the average consumer. To solidify this concept more clearly, here is a list of various companies and their credit score ranges:

- FICO: 300-850

- CreditXpert: 300-900

- ScoreSense: 350-850

- Equifax Credit Score: 360-840

These ranges demonstrate how widely credit lenders can differ in terms of how they calculate credit scores. It's important to know these details in the company that you choose to work with before committing to a company. The next sections will generalize what the different scores mean and their limitations, rather than committing to the exact ranges of a specific company. We will go from looking at the worst ranges of credit, to examining the best ranges.

Credit Score Range: 300 to 599

A credit score anywhere between 300 to slightly lower than 600 is definitely not seen favorably in the eyes of a lender. A credit score falling within this range is usually referred to as "very bad" within the credit industry. In addition to being unable to get a loan with a credit score of this type, it might also be hard to get a job. If an employer has a policy that consists of examining a credit score prior to hiring, the likelihood that you will get the job is very small. If your credit is this low, the best advice is to focus on reducing your debt, reducing the number of collection agencies that are after you through negotiating tactics, and making your current payments on time should be your primary focus. People in this category have burdened themselves with bankruptcy and repossessions. Other advice for people in this category include hiring a credit counselor and creating a long term plan for how you're going to grow your credit.

Credit Score Range: 600 to 649

Instead of "very bad", this category is reserved for people with simply "bad" credit. No one wants to be in this category. This is also known as the "subprime" category, meaning that credit lenders will still considering lending to you, but you will be offered loans at extremely high interest rates because your borrowing history is unfavorable. Hardships that fall on people within this category include poor payment histories, bankruptcy filings, and uncontrollably high amounts of credit card debt. Someone who wants to rise up from this type of poor credit may need to find a co-signer in order to have any hopes of doing so. Similar to the last category, mortgage companies will probably refuse to deal with you if your credit score falls within this range. Insurance companies, while they will offer you a small portion of their services, will only do so at extremely high rates.

Credit Score Range: 650 to 699

This credit range is commonly referred to as "acceptable" or "average". It's sort of the middle of the road, and people with this type of credit score are either pulling themselves up and out of extremely desolate financial times or are just seeing some hard times and might be headed towards even worse financial conditions.

This range usually prompts credit lenders to look into exactly why your credit score is within this range. While the first two categories that we discussed can be interpreted as points of no return, a credit lender might look at a score within this category and realize that a person has this type of credit score due to an unforeseen circumstance. For example, if you are in this category because you are frequently making late payments, a credit lender is less likely to give you a low interest rate than if you are in this category because you agreed to be someone's co-signer and they wrecked your credit history. The good news is, if you work hard to get this credit improved, it should only take a few months for it to go from "average" to "good".

Credit Score Range: 700 to 749

If you achieve this credit score, you are within the "good" range of credit scores. It's likely that you will be approved for most loans that you apply to receive, although you might not receive the lowest interest rates available. Some factors that can keep you from going from a designation of "good" to "great" include having a bit too much credit card debt, having a history of a few late payments, and perhaps having to deal with a collection agency in the past. The good news is that you shouldn't have any trouble securing employment.

Credit Score Range: 750 and Above

If you have a credit score of 750 0or higher, you've reached the big leagues. You will be offered the lowest interest rates and are considered to have an "excellent" credit score. If you fall within this category, you don't have to worry about not being approved for any type of loan for which you apply. What differentiates people who have a credit score between 750 and 800 and those who have one that is between 800 and higher is that the people in the former category may have missed a payment here or there or may have a strange employment history.

Conclusion

Knowing is only half the battle, the other half is action or application of knowledge. Merely learning about how to increase your credit score won't help you increase it. You'll need to apply what you learn. And when I say apply, I'm not talking about applying everything in one fell swoop. No, that's not a wise way to proceed. By applying what you learned a.s.a.p. I mean start applying one or two key lessons at a time – take baby steps. That way, you won't feel overwhelmed so you can gradually accumulate small victories that'll enable you to achieve much bigger ones when it comes to increasing your credit score.

Here's to your success my friend! Cheers!

www.ingramcontent.com/pod-product-compliance
Lightning Source LLC
Chambersburg PA
CBHW071208210326
41597CB00016B/1733